HANDBOOK

TO THE

JEYPORE MUSEUM

HANDBOOK

TO THE

JEYPORE MUSEUM

BY

THOMAS HOLBEIN HENDLEY,

ILLUSTRATED BY

W. GRIGGS

GYAN

Published by

Gyan Publishing House
5, Ansari Road
Daryaganj, New Delhi-110002
Phone: 011-47034999, 9811692060
E-mail: books@gyanbooks.com

Distribution Network
gyanbooks.com
India, USA, Canada, UK, Australia, France

ISBN: 978-93-6280-917-9 (PB)

First Published, 1895

2nd Impression 2023

Printed at: Gyan Press, Delhi.

HANDBOOK TO THE JEYPORE MUSEUM
AUTHORS: THOMAS HOLBEIN HENDLEY, Illustrator: W. GRIGGS

HANDBOOK

TO THE

JEYPORE MUSEUM

BY

T. HOLBEIN HENDLEY, C.I.E.

HANDBOOK

TO THE

JEYPORE MUSEUM

BY

THOMAS HOLBEIN HENDLEY, C.I.E.,

Brigade-Surgeon-Lieut.-Colonel, Indian Medical Department;

Honorary Secretary of the Jeypore Museum and of the Exhibition of Indian Art Metal Work, Imperial Institute, 1892;

President of the Art Conference, Lahore, 1894;

Chairman of the Executive Committee of the Jeypore Exhibition, 1883;

Governor and Member of the Executive Council of the Imperial Institute, 1891-92, &c., &c.

Author of several works on Indian Art.

WITH SIXTEEN FULL-PAGE ILLUSTRATIONS, PHOTO-CHROMO-LITHOGRAPHED

BY

W. GRIGGS

FROM WATER-COLOUR DRAWINGS BY INDIAN ARTISTS.

Calcutta:

PRINTED BY THE CALCUTTA CENTRAL PRESS COMPANY, LIMITED,

5 COUNCIL HOUSE STREET.

1895.

Short Notes for the information and guidance of Visitors to Jeypore.

Forms of application to visit Amber, the old capital of the State, and the Jeypore Palace, are kept at the hotels, or can be obtained from the Head Clerk at the Residency Office. The date and hour of the proposed visits should be entered on the form, as well as the number of persons in the party. It should then be sent to the Office of the Resident, who will forward in return, as early as possible, a pass granting permission to see the different places.

If the Resident is not in the station, the form should be sent to the Residency Surgeon, and, in the absence of both, to the Private Secretary of H. H. The Maharaja.

As a rule, H. H. The Maharaja has been good enough to undertake to send an elephant for each party to the foot of the pass which leads to Amber. On public festivals, however, of which a list is hung up at the hotels, the elephants are required for processional purposes, and will not therefore be available for the use of visitors, who will be able to make other arrangements, and so not be disappointed at the last moment.

The following is a list of the PRINCIPAL PLACES OF INTEREST :—

Places for which permission to visit is required.

AMBER, the old capital.—Application should, if possible, be made on the previous day. The morning is the best time for a visit.

JEYPORE PALACE, including Stables and old Observatory.

Other places of interest.

ALBERT HALL and the MUSEUM in the RAM NEWAS GARDEN.—Open free from sunrise to sunset on weekdays. From sunrise to 10 A.M., and 3 P.M. to sunset on Sundays.

SCHOOL OF INDUSTRIAL ART.—10 A.M. to 5 P.M. in winter. Sunrise to 10 or 11 A.M. in summer.

COLLECTION OF TIGERS.—In the City.

The GULTA.—A pass with picturesque tanks and temples.

The RAM NEWAS GARDENS and ZOOLOGICAL COLLECTION.—H. H. the Maharaja's band plays here every Monday afternoon, and the fern house and Museum are lighted up after the music ceases.

The COLLEGE and CENTRAL JAIL can be seen by visitors on presentation of cards to the Heads of those institutions.

The City gates are opened for vehicles about daybreak, and are closed two hours after sunset. Foot passengers can enter or leave up to 11 P.M.

CHURCHES.

CHURCH OF ENGLAND—*All Saints.* Divine Service at 6 P.M. every Sunday in winter, and at 6-30 P.M. or 7-0 P.M. in the hot season. On the fourth Sunday in every month in the morning in addition at hours advertised in the hotels.

ROMAN CATHOLIC CHAPEL of the *Sacred Heart of Jesus.*—Mass at 8 A.M. in winter, and at 7 A.M. in summer. Benediction at 5-30 P.M. in winter, and at 6-30 P.M. in summer.

There is a branch of the United Presbyterian Mission at Jeypore.

HOSPITALS AND DISPENSARIES.

THE MAYO HOSPITAL, for in- and out-patients, is situated at the north-east angle of the public gardens near the Sanganir Gate of the City.

There are three other Dispensaries in the town, and a Chemist's Shop in the Amber Chauk or Western Central Square of the City.

HOTELS.

There are two good hotels at Jeypore:—

(1.) THE DAK BUNGALOW or RUSTOM HOTEL, at which travellers can make their own arrangements for food, or be provided with everything, as in the best hotels, by the resident manager. The building is about a mile from the station, or nearly half way to the City, and it stands near the Government Telegraph Office.

(2.) THE KAISAR-I-HIND HOTEL.—It is situated about a quarter of a mile to the south-east of the Railway Station, a little beyond the Post Office, which is within railway limits. It is under efficient management. Carriages and guides can be procured at both hotels.

(3.) There are two principal Serais outside the City: one near the Railway Station belonging to Thakur Futteh Singh ; the other, outside the Sanganir Gate, to Seth Nath Mal.

LIBRARY.

THE PUBLIC LIBRARY, which contains more than ten thousand works, is open also as a free reading-room during daylight, except for three hours in the middle of the day. It is in the centre of the City, in front of the Tripolia or ordinary entrance of the Palace.

SANGANIR.

The old town of Sanganir, eight miles south of Jeypore, on the Tonk Road, contains a very fine old Jain temple in the style of the more famous shrines at Mount Aboo.

GENERAL NOTES.

For visitors who remain one clear day at Jeypore, the best plan would probably be to devote the morning from daybreak for about four hours to Amber, and after breakfast to see the Museum, the School of Art, the Palace, Stables, with the Observatory and the Tigers, finishing with a second visit to the Gardens and the Museum, from the top of which a beautiful view of the City and neighbourhood can be obtained.

To those who can spare a second day, a more leisurely visit to the Museum and School of Art is suggested, and excursions might be made to the Ghat—a pass in the hills or to the Gulta.

The institutions can also be examined. The best time to see the town and its inhabitants is for about an hour or two before dusk. The most picturesquely dressed crowds will be found near the Manak Chowk and in the main streets between the Tripolia and the Sanganir Gate, which is close to the Mayo Hospital.

The following are the

PRINCIPAL INDUSTRIAL ARTS OF JEYPORE:—

1. Enamel on gold.

2. Garnet Jewellery. The best Garnets in the country are found in or near the Jeypore State.

3. Stone images.

4. Felt rugs or Numdahs.

5. Arms of all kinds.

6. Lacquered toys and bracelets.

7. Semi-translucent porcelain.

8. Chintzes or dyed cotton cloths from Sanganir near Jeypore and other dye fabrics.

9. Jewellery of all kinds.

10. Engraved and hammered brass ware.

11. Bazar Pictures.

12. *Papier mâche* figures and heads of men of different castes.

13. Gold and Silver Lace.

The PRINCIPAL JEWELLERS are Phul Chand, son of Kasinath, Gopalji-ka-rasta, and Sobhag Chand, Ghi-wala-ka-rasta.

ARMS AND BRASS WARE.

Nur Baksh, Jawahri Bazar and Ajmere Gate.

Meera Buksh, Jawahri Bazar.

Curios generally—School of Art, Ajmere Gate Road; Messrs. Zoroaster & Co., Bhumia-ka-rasta.

Stone Images, &c.—Suraj Buksh, Tripolia Bazar.

Garnet Dealers—Sarbsukh, Jawahri, Gopalji-ka-rasta.

LIST OF PLATES.

INDEX OF CHAPTERS.

I. JEYPORE MUSEUM.

HANDBOOK
TO THE
JEYPORE MUSEUM.

CHAPTER I.

INTRODUCTION.

THE Museum was opened in temporary rooms in the City of Jeypore on August 21st, 1881, by Colonel Walter, Officiating Agent to the Governor-General in Rajputana.

The collections were transferred to their present home at the close of the year 1886, and the new institution was formally inaugurated by Sir Edward Bradford, at that time Agent to the Governor-General, on February 21st, 1887. The Museum was founded and is maintained by H. H. Sir Sawai Madho Singh, Bahadur, G.C.S.I., Maharaja of Jeypore.

It is open, without admission charge, to visitors of all classes, between dawn and dusk on week days, and for a few hours in the morning and afternoon on Sundays. Once a week (at present on Monday) it is lighted with gas for an hour or two after sunset.

The building in which the Museum collections are deposited is styled the Albert Hall, in honour of H. R. H. the Prince of Wales, who laid the foundation-stone on February 6th, 1876.

Shortly before the date of the visit of His Royal Highness to Jeypore, Rao Bahadur Kantee Chunder Mookerjee, C.I.E., was consulted by the Chief as to whether the erection of such a building would fitly commemorate that most important event in the history of the State. This appears to have been the first idea of the project. Before the death of H. H. the Maharaja, Sir Sawai Ram Singh Bahadur, G.C.S.I., in September 1880, the foundations and plinth were well advanced.

The superstructure has been erected during the reign, and at the expense, of H. H. Sir Sawai Madho Singh Bahadur, G.C.S.I., the present head of the State.

Colonel Jacob, C.I.E., Superintending Engineer at Jeypore, is the architect.

The Albert Hall stands in the Ramnewas or Public Gardens of Jeypore, which are conveniently situated between its two principal gates on the south side of the city about two miles east of the railway station.

The building is designed in the Indo-Saracenic style, with the modifications necessary to adapt it for use as a modern public edifice.

It stands on a high plinth, to which access is gained by broad flights of steps. In front is a large open hall or portico with a deep and partially-enclosed verandah all round. This ante-room opens into the main hall, which is used for holding meetings or State dinners and for lecturing purposes.

The hall is separated from the Museum proper by a corridor, and on either side of it there are courts which have fountains in the midst and open colonnades all round them.

The Museum itself is entered by a revolving turnstile at the south-east angle of the eastern court.

The Industrial Art exhibits are arranged in the rooms and corridors on the ground floor, and the Natural History and Educational collections will be found on the upper floor, and may be most conveniently examined by commencing at the west staircase. Jeypore has always been famous throughout North India for the beauty of its carving in stone; but as the architect relied upon this important feature for the chief ornamentation of his building, it has not been thought necessary to make a special collection to illustrate this local art, but rather to direct the visitor's attention to the principal decorative examples in the edifice itself as he passes from one part of it to another.

The building can be lighted at night with gas of very clear and pure quality, which is manufactured from kerosine oil. The collections in the larger rooms are arranged in cases of the South Kensington type. Most of them have been fitted with plate glass.

They were chiefly supplied by Mr. Wimbridge, of Bombay, but the long and small cases in the corridors on the upper floor were made by Messrs. Richardson & Cruddas, of the same city. Most of the wall frames and two large cases in the Central Hall of the Museum were constructed in Jeypore by Mr. A. Tellery and the Museum carpenters, and prove that local workmen are quite capable of doing good joiner's work when under skilled supervision.

The floors were covered with dark maroon-coloured *munj* matting, and the smaller cases are lined with paper of the same tint, because it serves as the best foil for the exhibits.

The fittings of the larger ones are covered with Turkey-red cotton cloth, because the woollen material which was formerly employed was rapidly destroyed by insects.

Durries from the Jeypore Jail have been used in some of the galleries, and will shortly be put down in all the rooms instead of matting.

The rooms are well ventilated from skylights, which are regulated by a special arrangement patented by the architect.

On the floor of the ladies' room there is a beautiful old Persian carpet, about 280 years old. It is believed that it was brought from Herat by Maharaja Man Singh, of Jeypore, who was the friend of Akbar, and for some time Governor of Kabul.

ANTE-ROOM.

The upper part of the walls has been divided into panels, on which have been painted the coat-of-arms of Jeypore, and a series of full-sized portraits of the principal Rulers of the State since 1503.

The latter were copied from what are presumed to be authentic, and for the most part contemporary, pictures, and are therefore extremely interesting as showing examples of different styles of dress, and the personal peculiarities of men of past generations who were in some instances very distinguished.

The principal Chiefs are Prithi Raj, the 17th Ruler of Jeypore, twelve of whose sons became the ancestors of as many great families of Jeypore (A.D. 1503 to 1528).

Bhagwant Das, the friend of the Emperor Akbar, whose life he had saved (1574 to 1590).

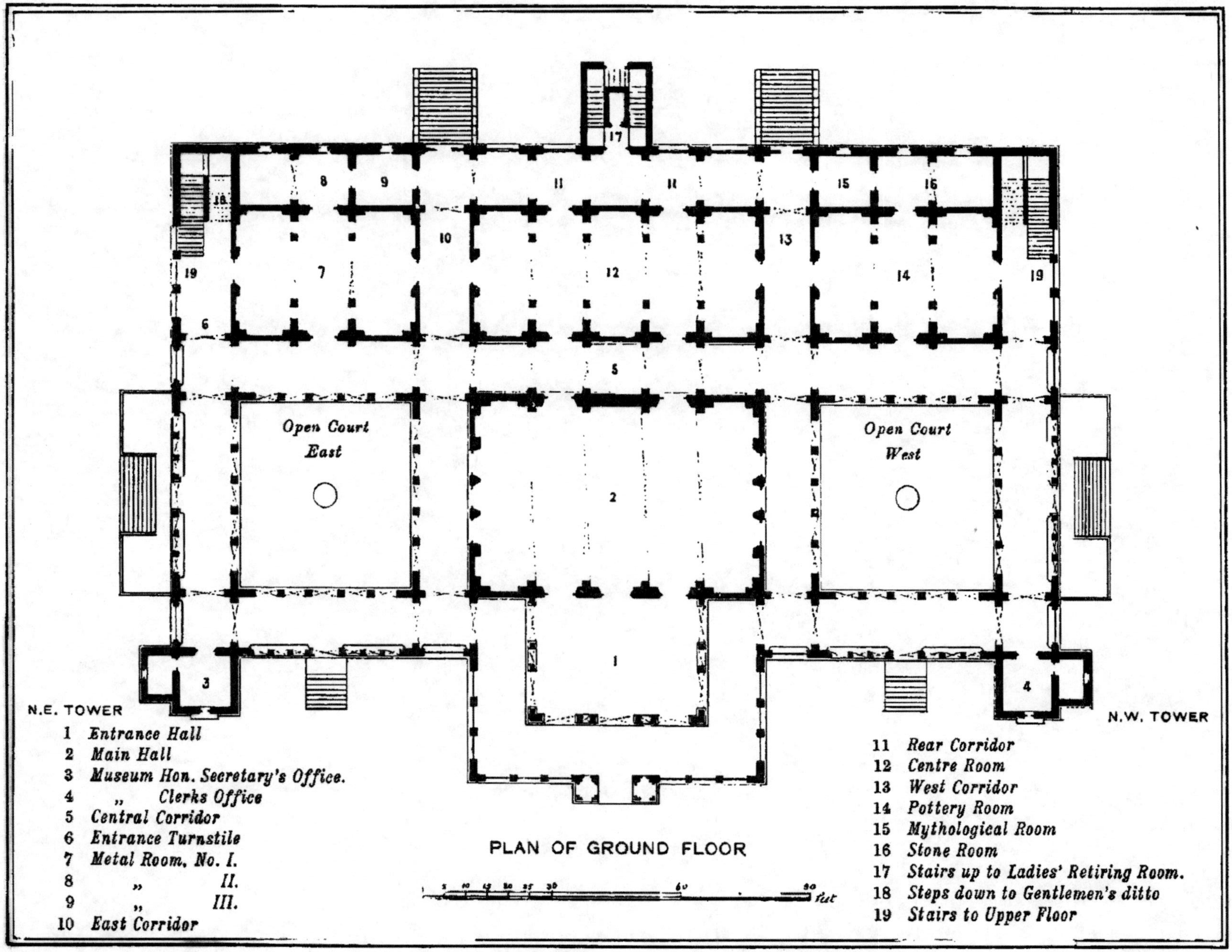

II. JEYPORE MUSEUM. PLAN OF GROUND FLOOR.

Man Singh, the conqueror of Orissa, and commander of 7,000 horse, a position above all Mohamedan officers of the Crown. He was at different times Viceroy of Bengal, Behar, the Deccan, and Kabul (1590 to 1615).

Jey Singh I, commander of 6,000 horse, a wise and powerful prince (1622 to 1668),

Sawai Jey Singh II, the founder of Jeypore, a famous astronomer, and a great general as well as consummate politician, who not only built the observatories at Jeypore, Delhi, Mathura, Benares, and Ujain, and reformed the Indian calendar, but was stated by some historians to have held the fate of the empire in his own hands (1700 to 1744).

Sawai Isri Singh, his son, under whom the Mahrattas first obtained a footing in Rajputana (1744 to 1751).

Sawai Madho Singh, another and more valiant son, whose bravery, however, did not suffice to prevent his State from being overrun by the predatory armies of the Mahrattas (1751 to 1768).

Sawai Jagat Singh II, with whom the first treaty of alliance with the British power in 1818 was formed (1803 to 1818).

Sir Sawai Ram Singh, G.C.S.I., who secured a well-deserved reputation for his enlightenment, his encouragement of art and learning, and his loyalty, as well as for his devotion to the paramount power (1835 to 1880).

And lastly, Sir Sawai Madho Singh II, G.C.S.I., thirty-fifth Maharaja of Jeypore and present head of the Kachhawa clan of Rajputs.

Paintings such as these are prepared by a kind of fresco process. The walls are plastered with a very carefully made coat of fine lime, which is dressed with as much oil as they are capable of absorbing, and is then covered with repeated layers of oxide of lead, each successive coat being carefully smoothed and burnished.

The picture is afterwards painted with oil pigments, and when finished is very durable, and does not peel off or perish if protected from the direct action of the sun and rain.

The visitor should first walk round the corridors and squares in order to examine the external walls of the rooms. He will notice that Colonel Jacob has inscribed above the arches of the courts most instructive mottoes from celebrated oriental classics, English translations of which will be found on panels inside the corridors opposite to them.

The remaining outer walls are also covered with paintings, which are intended to represent all those influences which may be supposed to have been at work in the formation of the Indo-Persian or present prevailing school of Indian art. They are prepared, in the same manner as the portraits of the Chiefs, by the State artists, who are the professional, if not in all cases the natural, descendants of the men who worked for the great Moghuls.

In the centre behind the principal hall there is a series of six paintings of subjects described in the Mahabharata and Ramayana, the great Indian epics. They are reproductions, on a large scale, of the illustrations of a copy of the Razmnamah or the Persian version of those epics which belonged to, and was prepared for, Akbar the Great, 300 years ago, by the best artists of his time, and which, therefore, represent the Indo-Persian school at its best. The original book is one of the chief treasures of the Jeypore family.

On the ground in front of these pictures are a number of casts from the Indo-Bactrian figures, now in the Lahore Museum, and some others of Hindi character from the caves of Amarnath in the Bombay Presidency. It is very interesting to compare the almost pure and refined Greek art of the earlier examples of the first series with the conventional, and somewhat inelegant, or even grotesque, Hindu figures, or with the characteristic, formal, and rather childish Indo-Persian drawings, in which two or three incidents are represented at once, and in which there is little attempt at Chiaroscuro, and no perspective, though there are much delicacy of touch and beautiful colouring, after the manner of the Byzantine school or of the mediæval miniatures.

Broadly speaking, the paintings on the right represent the Turanian ideas, and those on the left the Aryan or Western. Thus on the east wall of the Great Hall we have two Egyptian subjects:—The first representing Rameses III, in his chariot, accompanied by his tame lion, in which the spectator is struck by the skill with which the artist has delineated action and power; the second, a characteristic processional picture from Thebes.

A little beyond we come to a picture in which a mandarin and his retinue are seen crossing a bridge of boats. It is the work of a Chinese painter.

In a second frame we find a Japanese artist's idea of a grand battue of animals on the plain before the sacred mountain of Fusiyama, and a little beyond are restorations of a palace at Nimroud and of a *Ziggurat* * or Temple of the Seven Spheres at Borsippa(?), and on the walls of the staircase the winged Lion and Bull of Assyria. These are illustrative of Babylonian and Assyrian art.

Returning to the west, we have, on the outer side walls of the Great Hall, two celebrated subjects:—

First, the battle of Issus from the mosaic in the House of the Faun at Pompeii, which has been looked upon by many authorities as the greatest masterpiece of the Græco-Roman school that has come down to us.

Second, another famous study, a fresco from Herculaneum, *viz.*, the desertion of Ariadne by Theseus after she had aided him in the destruction of the Minotaur, and, on the front walls near the portico, portions of the famous Archer frieze from Susa, which was discovered by Mons. Dieulafoy in 1885. These represent soldiers of the Immortal Guard of the Great Persian King.

On the north wall of the main building close by are two very fine subjects from the caves of Ajunta, one representing the conquest of Ceylon, the other strangers adoring Buddha. They date from the fifth century A.D., and both give a grand idea of Buddhist art.

A little further, the following important studies will be noted:—

First, the Emperor Justinian and his attendants, from a mosaic in the Church of San Vitale at Ravenna, which was erected between 528 and 547 A.D. in the reign of that great sovereign himself while St. Eulalie was Bishop. This is a good example of the Byzantine or formal school, which had so much to do in a direct way with the formation of the modern Persian and Arabian styles of art.

On the next wall is an enlarged reproduction from the Arundel Society's chromolithograph of a painting by Giotto, the first and mightiest artist of the thirteenth century, who represents the revival of art, and whose influence long left its impress upon the Italian school of his age (1276-1336).

---

* Ziggurat restored according to probabilities (Perrot and Chipiez).

The subject is St. Francis before Pope Honorius III; the original is in the upper church at Assisi in Italy. On the side of the west staircase, there is an Etruscan painting, which decidedly shows Greek influence. Etruria, in which the Etruscans lived, roughly corresponds with Tuscany in Italy, and some authorities have thought that this country is the home of modern European art. Pictures from early Greek vases fill up the opposite wall.

All the pictures have been chosen as characteristic examples of their respective styles, and have been surrounded by gilded frames, to indicate that they are to be regarded as pictures, and not as portions of the decoration of the building. They have been carefully executed by the State artists from copies which were made especially for the purpose principally in London and Bombay.

THE GREAT HALL.

This fine hall is used for various public purposes; for example, for receptions, lectures, magic lantern entertainments, and dinners. It is floored with wooden boards, and folding chairs in sufficient numbers are stored in the cellars, which are brought up when required.

The visitor should particularly observe the fine red marble shafts, and the arabesque plaster ornament round the different recesses, which has been copied from the Agra and Delhi, Mohamedan, edifices, and also the dado of painted flowers done after the manner of the jewelled work in the Tajmahal. Two of the upper windows have been filled with coloured glass, to represent the Gods of the Sun and Moon driving their chariots. The outlines are formed by bands of plaster in the oldest style of glass window decoration, which is really a form of glass mosaic.

The two principal Rajput clans are said to be descended from the Sun and Moon, and are consequently known as the Suraj and Chandra Vansi, or solar and lunar races respectively.

The Chiefs of Jeypore, Udaipur, and Jodhpore are of the former line, and those of Jeysulmere and Karauli of the latter.

In the centre of the south wall there is a portrait of H. R. H. the Prince of Wales, which was copied, with the special permission of His Royal Highness, from a painting by Professor Angeli. The original is now in Marlborough House. Near it are three large metal shields: on the circular one in the centre is portrayed, on a number of silver-plated plaques, the story of the great Horse Sacrifice or Ashwamedha, which took place in the early history of India; and on the oval shields adjacent, in like manner, the principal events narrated in the Mahabharata and Ramayana are depicted. The incidents are for the most part faithful reproductions in repoussé of original designs from Akbar's Razmnamah (see page 3). The arrangement and general scheme are by the author of this handbook, and the work has been carried out by Ganga Baksh, Khati, one of the best artists in brass in Jeypore. They may be looked upon as "masterpieces of manipulative skill of the Indian artists in metal work."—Sir G. Birdwood.*

* As these shields are intended to illustrate the technical skill of the workmen of the present day, modern processes are used where desirable.

CHAPTER II.

THE MUSEUM.

THE ground floor of the principal block of the building is devoted to the Industrial Art section. It is entered on the east by a revolving turnstile. The first room is set apart for metal ware of all kinds, including lace and textiles that are enriched with gold or silver wire.

THE METAL ROOM.

In this and all other parts of the Museum, the articles, which require most minute examination, are displayed in the centre cases, and objects, whose interest consists chiefly in their form or place in the classification, or in which the details of arrangement are not very remarkable, are placed on the side shelves. Brocades, and fabrics enriched with metal, have been arranged in a decorative manner in the recess cases in this room, and some of the small specimens are shown in revolving pillar frames.

The carved panels, on the marble columns, which support the galleries, are copied from pillars at Kankraoli in Meywar, and the string and band patterns from old buildings chiefly near Delhi. The marble brackets, supporting the balcony over the doorways, are taken from the Arab Serai, an old building near Delhi.

They are beautiful examples of decorative art, and the little delicate pendants which hang between the columns are singularly graceful. They were copied from the old temples on Mount Abu.

The general arrangement of the collections is systematic rather than geographical, though some attempt has been made to combine both plans, which is less impossible than would be thought likely, as each division of the Indian Empire has, on the whole, its own fairly marked style of art-work ; that, for example, of North India, showing most traces of both ancient and modern Persian, and of Assyrian, or of Central Asian, and even of Greek influence ; that of Bengal and Burmah of their art kinship with further Asia, while the work of the Western provinces bears strong relation to a connection with Arabia and Europe, and more particularly, perhaps, with Portugal, Holland, and, even more remotely, with Rome and Greece again, with all of which countries there is a history of trade communication.

The arts of the south are of the most archaic and truly peninsular character.

The truth of these remarks is adequately illustrated by the numerous specimens which have been brought together in the metal room. The visitor will probably leave with the impression that Indian art has a substratum of all the styles he has ever seen ; that, although there is a trace throughout of something peculiar to India in almost everything, the underlying motive and force are not of this country. Everywhere decoration is carried to its extreme limits, and surfaces are elaborately covered with ornament, but there is a want of simplicity, and consequent boldness and character ,which is pretty generally felt. In short, the beautiful objects are for the most part such as would be made by clever, hereditary craftsmen, with wonderful dexterity of touch and keen colour sense, but without sufficient knowledge or mental education to grasp a great law or to originate a truly noble work.

In this room, as in most of the others, the first case contains what may be termed a

III. JEYPORE MUSEUM. INTERIOR.

synoptic or key collection. It is therefore suggested that the visitor should begin by studying its contents and then proceed to examine the other cases in the order of their numbers. Small indicating hands (coloured red) have also been placed on the cases and frames to point out the order in which the objects should be inspected, and the labels give all information regarding the articles which is notf ound in the handbook, and which is really necessary to understand them. Vernacular descriptions are being prepared, but are not so full as the English ones.

It has not been thought necessary to minutely describe every specimen in the Museum, but only to dwell upon what is most suggestive or interesting. Anything of special value is distinguished by a red star, and has its label also marked in the same manner. This is the plan which was adopted by the author in his handbook to the Indian Art Metalwork Exhibition of the Imperial Institute in London in 1892. The following extract from that handbook will still further indicate the lines on which it is proposed to write the present work:—

"Instead of adopting the usual course of preparing a detailed catalogue of the objects exhibited, it has been thought that it would most enhance the interest of the collection to label every article explicitly, to mark the most suggestive and valuable exhibits in a prominent manner (*viz.*, with a *red star* on the descriptive card), and to produce in pamphlet form a brief account of these and of the different manufactures."

SYNOPTIC CASE NO. 1.

The best decorative work in metal was in former times almost always applied to the ornamentation of arms and armour.

The synoptic case is therefore for the most part filled with such articles, though there are a few exceptions.

A portrait of H. H. Maharaja Sir Sawai Madho Singh Bahadur, G.C.S.I., has been placed in the front of the case, as he is not only the head of the Kachhawa chivalry, but the founder and sole supporter of the Museum.

It will be convenient in the next instance to draw attention to the specimens of damascening in gold. Of this there are two kinds, *viz.*, the *tah-i-nishan* or true damascening, in which gold wire is forced into deep channels cut in steel, and the false or *koft* work. In the latter, gold wire, or even leaf, are only made to adhere to the ground metal by means of slight grooves with filing and polishing, or even through the medium of some adhesive substance.

Of the koft work, the following are good examples:—Nos. 2, 3, 4, and 28. A cuirass of four pieces, forming the four mirrors or *char-aina* of the Persians, with a pair of gauntlets and a helmet, made by Futeh Din of Sialkot. These pieces took the prize for gold damascening at the Jeypore Exhibition of 1883. No. 19, a shield; No. 22, a salver with Arabic inscription, in which both gold and silver wire have been used in the manner termed Ganga Jamni, that is in imitation of the junction at Allahabad of the clear water of the Jamna with the muddy stream of the Ganges river; No. 30, a circular tray; No. 31, a salver with judicious contrast of ground and finely drawn ornament; and No. 32, a shield from the School of Art, Jeypore.

Some of the *tah-i-nishan* examples are very fine, particularly No. 6, a Hindu thrusting dagger or *katar*, which is enriched with beautifully executed scenes from animal life. Nos. 7 to 11, five sword hilts from the Jeypore armoury. Nos. 14 to 17, daggers from the same place; and Nos. 12 and 13, two specimens from Sirohi, in which the wire is remarkably thick, and the work good. Sirohi is a small, but very ancient state, near Mount Abu. It was famous for its weapons even in the days of Pliny. The salver (No. 20) won the prize at the Simla Exhibition for the bold manner in which the floral ornament was executed.

In the front of the case will be noticed a large brass salver (No. 35), a fine example of the repoussé work in brass for which Jeypore has of late become rather famous. In the centre the Sun god is shown seated in his chariot, and round him are ranged, in two concentric circles, the signs of the Zodiac and the lunar asterisms. Raghunath the maker is perhaps one of the two best workmen in Jeypore. In the ancient Hindu astronomy the earth was the centre of the System, but such an anachronism would not have been possible in this city since the days of Jey Singh, the founder of Jeypore and the greatest astronomer of modern India. No. 36 is an iron helmet from the Maharaja's armoury. The band is divided into compartments, which are pierced into mythological figures. There are traces of enamel in some places. Good work in iron is somewhat rarely found in North India.

Amongst the swords and daggers are numerous illustrations of the employment, in various ways, of different materials to enrich them. The sheath of sword No. 51 from Cutch has mounts with embossed silver patterns. The hilt of sword No. 53 from the same place is encrusted with imitation gems. Precious stones of little value, or in thin scales, are used so as to secure the greatest amount of show and glitter for a trifling outlay. The sheaths of swords and daggers are generally made of two pieces of such a wood as that of the *Ailanthus excelsa* tree, and require careful handling, as they are only united by the figured cloth or brocade that covers them, which of course is easily cut by the sharp blade within.

The Indian sword hilt with large pommel and knuckle guard (Nos. 7 to 10) is usually made separately from the blade. The Persian pistol-shaped hilt (an old form, found amongst relics of ancient Egypt and Assyria) is frequently made up of the tang of the blades and of two side pieces of walrus ivory (No. 57), or the dagger may have its hilt of jade (No. 60), of crystal, or stone of different kinds, or of iron, or gold set with jewels, or be richly enamelled. Nos. 77 to 79 are curious powder horns in the form of the heads of animals. Lastly, there is a model of a *chhatri* or cenotaph, such as is erected over the spot on which the body of a Rajput prince is burnt. Fine examples of such buildings are found in different styles in most of the Rajputana capitals.

The series of *chhatries* at Gehtore, the cremation-place of the Chiefs of Jeypore, is particularly interesting, as it illustrates the architectural history of the place since the beginning of the eighteenth century, and especially the different forms assumed by the pendentives of domes. The cenotaphs at Mundore near Jodhpore are more like temples with spires.

Those of the Maha Sati at Ahar in the Udaipur valley are the most picturesque and extensive, as not only are the Chiefs commemorated, but the principal Nobles and Officials also.

Recess Case No. 2.

The two *saries* or women's veils at the top of this case (Nos. 81 and 82) were made in Ajmere, and are stamped in imitation gold. Such cloths are worn by the poor at weddings and other festivals, and there is a large manufacture of, and trade in, them throughout Rajputana. The more wealthy use fabrics stamped with the precious metals.

Below them are leather shields from the Jeypore State, which are variously ornamented with painted floral and figure designs and metal bosses (Nos. 83 to 85). Such shields were formerly carried by Rajput soldiers, huntsmen, and official peons or messengers, but, with the more extended sale of firearms, are gradually being disused. There is, however, a considerable demand for them by tourists for decorative purposes. The best in the Jeypore State are perhaps made at Uniara. Some of a superior kind come from Shahpura in Meywar. The case contains a number of specimens of Moradabad ware, of which there are several kinds, all having a groundwork of brass.

In the first or *sada* (Nos. 87 to 91-94), the brass is covered with tin, through which a design is cut, so that the patterns are yellow on a white ground.

In the *Syah Kalam* variety (Nos. 95 to 96 and 103 to 117), according to Babu T. N. Mookerjee, the ground of the vessel is graven out, bringing into relief the floriated patterns. The depression in the ground is then filled with a black composition of lac, leaving the scrolls of a golden yellow colour. Red and green lacquers have lately been introduced both for ground and pattern, but in these variations inferiority of workmanship, which is too often observed in the present day, is perhaps most marked.

The oldest and best work is generally thought to be distinguished by bold and simple outlines.

The best specimens in the collection are Nos. 102, 103, 104, 106, 110 and 114. From Lucknow come examples of false Bidri work made in imitation of the true kind from Bidar in the Nizam's Territory (Nos. 97 to 102). This will be conveniently described later on, but reference may be made here to the variety of it, which is somewhat similar to the Moradabad ware, and is known by the modern name of *zarbuland* (raised work).

Wall Frames Nos. 3 and 8.

The textiles shown in the wall frames are of some interest. It will hardly be necessary to do more than refer to the hanging scrolls or *kaikomonas*, which are fair examples of the ingenuity and fertility of invention of the inhabitants of Japan (Nos. 118 and 123). Nos. 119 and 124 are examples of brocade, or cloth of gold—*kinkhwab* or *kincob*—from Ahmedabad. Some time ago, *kinkhwabs* were also made in Jeypore, but the principal centres for the manufacture are now Benares and Ahmedabad.

The demand for these beautiful fabrics is however diminishing with the increasing cheapness of European stuffs. The Ahmedabad designs are generally less striking and more minute than those from Benares, though the work is often very exquisite. The curse of the textile industries, *viz.*, the Aniline Dyes, bids fair, however, to ruin this the most glorious of them all. Some striking examples of this abomination are shown, but it is to be feared without any chance of horrifying either the manufacturers or their clients.

Recess Case No. 9.

I can only briefly note the contents of this case, which are principally domestic brass vessels from different parts of India. The most important are brass and copper articles from Poona. In them the ornamentation is chiefly in floral repoussé executed after the manner of the well-known silver Cutch ware, of which it is indeed a direct imitation in base metal (Nos. 143 to 151, &c.)

A few simple but well-shaped vessels, in white metal, from Bhilwarra, the commercial capital of Meywar or Udaipur, are worthy of remark. There is a large trade in them (Nos. 152 to 157 and 167 to 180). Nos. 158 and 159 are curious boxes which are filled with coloured powders, and perforated, in such a way that, when drawn along the ground, they make floral patterns round the spaces which are marked off for the guests at feasts. They are chiefly used by Mahrattas.

The adjacent photographs (Frame No. 12) of the Bell of St. Patrick, now in Dublin, will be of interest to the student, as much of the ornament seems to have had a common origin with that so often seen in Indian work.

Revolving Pillar Frame No. 13.

Benares Brocade (Nos. 186 to 201). These fabrics are very expensive, and as they are only sold by the piece or *than* of about nine yards in length, small specimens are not easily procurable. They are chiefly used for state garments for men. They are sold by weight.

Small Case No. 14.

Nos. 203 to 208 are examples of Bidri work which were presented to the Museum by H. H. the Nizam of Hyderabad. Sir G. Birdwood thus writes of this manufacture:—"At present the four chief seats of Bidri manufacture are Bidar itself, Lucknow in Oudh, Purneah and Moorshidabad in Bengal. The mode of manufacture is very nearly the same in all the places. The manufacture of Bidri ware is carried on under a system of division of labour, the different processes being generally performed by three classes of people, *viz.*, the moulder, the carver, and the inlayer. The moulder prepares the alloyed metal, casts the vessel, and turns it to its proper shape by his lathe. The carver engraves the pattern on the surface of the vessel, and the inlayer designs the patterns, inlays the ornament of gold or silver, and finally colours and polishes the article. A modified form of Bidri work, called *zarbuland,* is made at Lucknow, in which the patterns are slightly raised and not set even with the surface as in the ordinary Bidri ware.

"In Bidri, the metal ground is a compound of copper, lead, and tin, made black on the surface by dipping in a solution of sal ammoniac, saltpetre, salt, and blue vitriol. This alloy, after being first melted and cast, is turned in a lathe to complete the form which is usually that of an ordinary *surahi,* or water-goblet, or *hukah*-stand. Then the required pattern is graven over it and inlaid with silver, and finally the ground of the vessel is blackened and its silver ornamentation scoured to the brightest polish."

Sir George refers to the division of labour. This is very common in Indian work, so

10842

340

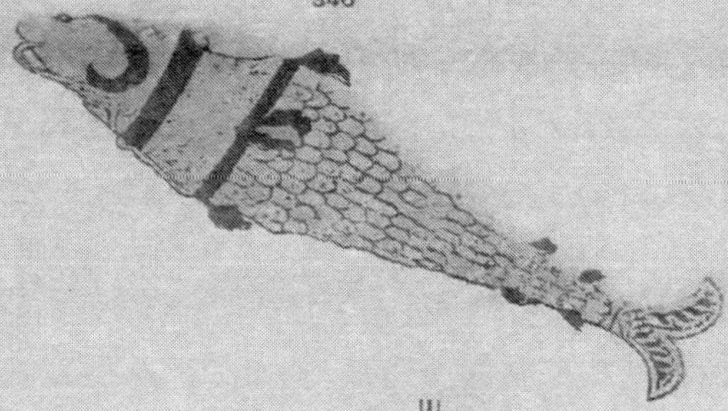

858

111

219

857

102

221

10842 SILVER PEACOCK. MATHURA
858 PAN BOX, PLATED BRASS. JEYPORE
340 SILVER FISH, OR ANTIMONY HOLDER. KARAKPUR, MONGHYR, BENGAL
219 WATER POT. IMARTI, TANJORE

857 GOURD-SHAPED CUP, SILVER GILT. KASHMIR
102 WATER BOTTLE, IMITATION BIDRI WORK. LUCKNOW
111 ROSE-WATER SPRINKLER. MORADABAD
221 SILVER PEPPER CASTOR. TRICHINOPOLY

XII MORADABAD AND BIDRI WARE.

much so, for example, in the case of enamelling, that the enameller cannot engrave the gold or prepare the design. In mediæval European work it was not usually so as one man could generally undertake all branches. Nos. 209 to 212 are specimens of Lucknow bidri. The patterns are much larger than in the Hyderabad ware and are encrusted on the composition.

Tanjore work (Nos. 213 to 219) is thus described by Dr. Bidie of Madras:—

"Ornamental work in copper and silver, brass and silver, and brass and copper, is made at Tanjore. It is of three kinds, namely, brass engraved, brass encrusted with copper, and copper encrusted with silver. Sometimes the brass and copper variety has also figures in tin introduced. In the graved brass work the first impressions are made with a die and by hammering. The work is then completed by cutting away the brass in the space between the figures, and giving it a granulated appearance with the graver. Finishing touches are also given to the figures. A *lotah* of the common globular shape is usually the subject of this kind of adornment, and the ordinary patterns embrace panels round the bilge with figures from the popular pantheon, and chaste conventional floral designs. Examined closely, the figures are seen to be coarsely finished, but the general effect at a little distance is excellent. In the copper and brass ware, the vessels are made of brass, and covered with figures of copper, which are fixed on the base metal by hammering, and a sort of dovetail union. After the crusts are put on and worked into shape, the figures are finished with a graver and a chisel. The designs on this ware are of the same character as those on the brass-graved vessels, but the figures are in bolder relief. This incrustation of copperware with silver figures is a modern adaptation of the older art of covering brass with copper figures, and the silver is attached to the copper by the same kind of junction as that employed for fixing copper on brass. But as the metals are more valuable, greater trouble is taken to secure a better finish, and an examination of the silver figures in first class work shows that more graver and less die or chisel work is used than in the case of copper or brass. The designs consist, as usual, of mythological figures and floral decorations, which, although in some cases rather crowded, have yet an excellent effect. In fact, profusion of ornament and intricate details are characteristic of all Hindu work from the embellishment of a temple to that of a lotah, and in the case of the Tanjore ware, age improves its appearance by deepening the hue of the copper, and toning down the colour of the silver. At Tirupati, North Arcot, district, various patterns are stamped on the brass, and into these figures thin plates of silver or copper are pressed, and apparently fixed by hammering the edges of the brass over the other metals so as to make a sort of dovetail. In fact, it is a rude kind of damascene work. The pieces of copper and silver thus used are introduced into the designs in a very irregular way, and the details of the figures, which are generally mythological or floral, are usually worked out by punched lines in imitation of engraving. The result is a certain barbaric splendour, but the general effect is bizarre in the extreme. The ware is chiefly made to be sold to the thousands of pilgrims who proceed to the famous shrine of Tirupati, and as they want something striking for their money, the designs do not usually receive much attention."

Incrustation is a very ancient method of ornamenting metal. The octagonal salver (18" long by 13" broad, No. 213) is perhaps the best example in this case. The ground is copper. In the centre are represented Krishna playing on the flute as the Lord of the Cowherds under the Kadamba (*Nauclea orientalis*) tree, while round him are the Gopis, or cowherdesses, and the Naga Kanyas or virgin daughters of the snake king of the Jamuna River.

This specimen cost Rs. 53-15, a fair indication of the value of the work.

In the body of piece No. 215 the ground is brass. That of the salver on which it rests is copper.

Nos. 221 to 225 are examples of silver *swami* work from Trichinopoly, so called because it is usually decorated with figures of South Indian gods in very high relief. It is applied to articles of European use.

No. 233, a slow-match holder, is perhaps the best example.

No. 220 is a set of cocoanut bracelets from Rutlam, which are grooved to receive thin plates of silver, some of which are embossed with simple floral patterns. This style of ornament is very common throughout India and of very ancient origin.

I found ivory and shell bracelets, grooved in this manner for silver or gold plates, twenty feet below the surface on an old Buddhist site near the Sambhur Lake. The rich women of the mercantile classes in Rajputana, and especially in Marwar, wear such bracelets enriched with massive plates of gold.

Nos. 226 to 235. These are specimens of silver and jewellery worn by Bedawin women on the shores of the Dead Sea, and were purchased there by Dr. Gordon Hull for the Museum. The resemblance to much of the Mohamedan jewellery of North India will be easily seen. The custom of making pilgrimages to Mecca from all parts of the Musalman world sufficiently explains the presence of Arab jewellery or *vice versâ* in India and Palestine.

To this practice of pilgrimage, so universal throughout the East, is due much of the confusion which enters into the investigation of the origin of Oriental manufactures, and the wholesale deportation of artists by such conquerors as Timur presents another difficulty, as will be seen later on.

CASE NO. 15.

This case contains articles of the greatest intrinsic value in the collection.

On the top shelf will be found a number of specimens of Jeypore enamel on gold, which Sir G. Birdwood describes as the master art of the world. It is of the variety known as champlevé, or that in which the plate or ground is excavated into little pits or depressions for the reception of the enamel colours.

These colours are oxides of metals, and they are made to adhere to the gold by heat. The outlines are formed by the gold of the plate, and the whole piece is carefully polished or burnished by agates after the oxides are fused.

The enamel is strong, and does not crack and fly off, as in many European examples of the art. As the colours, for the most part, adhere with different degrees of heat, they have to be applied separately, and those which melt at the lowest temperature are put on last of all.

There is great risk in preparing a large piece, which may be spoiled at any moment; hence the great value of enamel. The Jeypore work is chiefly noted for the fire and

233 BRACELET. (a) INSIDE OF DITTO. (b) OUTSIDE ORNAMENT
246 MANGO-SHAPED LOCKET OR KAIREE.
245 CHARM WORN BY PILGRIMS TO NATHDWARRA.
242 BROOCH.
248 FISH RING.
236 CUP.
237 BACK OF A NECKLACE.

VI. ENAMEL ON GOLD, JEYPORE.

beauty of its red hues. The artists are nearly all Sikhs, and it is supposed that they practised their art in the first place at Lahore. Many of the designs they most delight in are taken from the tile pictures on the outer walls of the palace of the great Moghuls in the fort at Lahore.

Many of the largest and most valuable pieces of Jeypore enamel now in existence are the property of H. M. the Queen-Empress, or of her sons, H. R. H. the Prince of Wales and H. R. H. the Duke of Edinburgh, and were exhibited in 1892 at the Imperial Institute. They included a beautiful native writing case in the shape of an Indian gondola, with the stern in the form of a peacock, and a number of fly whisks or *chauris* with handles of enamel, and plumes of the white tails of the yak or *Bos gruniens.* These latter, together with plumes of gold and peacock's feathers, termed Morchals, and a few other articles, varying in different courts, form the insignia of Indian royalty.

One large salver, the property of H. R. H. the Prince of Wales, took two years to manufacture. A very fine hookah, with appurtenances, also belongs to the Prince, and another of similar kind is owned by H. H. the Maharaja of Rewah, who sent it to the Jeypore Exhibition of 1883. Fairly good specimens of enamel are made at Delhi and Ulwar, but the colours from the former city are not as clear or pure as those of Jeypore, *e.g.*, the red is generally of a brownish tinge, as may be seen in the ordinary Delhi jewellery, in which large gold ornaments are usually enamelled on the inner and back surfaces. For further information reference should be made to the monograph on the subject by Col. Jacob and myself.*

No. 236 in the Museum, a cup with cover, is a fair specimen of the work of a good enameller, Ghoma Singh, a Sikh resident of Jeypore.

The backs of the plaques of the necklace (No. 237) are of the finest workmanship by the late Amar Singh, who was regarded as the best artist of his day in Jeypore.

The bracelet No. 239 terminates in the heads of two dragons or fabulous monsters, the *azdaha* of the Persians. The Sosan flowers or lilies on the top of the box No. 240 are in fine red enamel, the glory of the Jeypore work.

The favourite examples for European use are bracelets, such as Nos. 238 and 243, mango-shaped charms (No. 246), or whistles (Nos. 251 and 252), and a common Rajputana ornament (No. 245), a charm in the form of a plaque decorated on one side with the footmarks of Krishna, as worshipped at Nathdwarra in Meywar, and the words "Sri Nath" or the "Holy Lord," one of his titles, on the other.

The case contains other interesting objects, as follow:—

No. 253. A hemispherical silver cover or umbrella in the form of a Jain temple dome to suspend over an image, which is usually also Jain.

No. 254. Jewellers' scales formed of thin silver pans with a very delicate steel balance. The agate weights are placed beside them. To ensure accuracy of these weights, a small caste feast had to be given.

No. 255. A steel box containing a minute set of toilet instruments, termed *ganj*, made at Bahawalpur.

---

* "Jeypore Enamels," Lieut.-Colonel Jacob and Surgeon-Major Hendley. 1886. Griggs.

Nos. 256 and 257. Gold coins of Oerkes Okro and Vasudeva, Bactrian kings at the end of the second century A.D., are shown here as examples of ancient Indian metallurgy. They were coined, while Greek influence was, to a certain extent, still felt in the country.

Nos. 258 to 262. Silver and gold Burmese coins, made by native workmen.

Nos. 263 to 267. Medals awarded to the Museum at different exhibitions.

No. 268. A belt of quasi-enamel from Pertabgarh in Rajputana. In this work the ground is composed of green glass ; and small figures, chiefly representing sporting subjects, are strewn, as it were, upon it in fine gold. These figures are deposited in pits in the glass by a process which is so far a secret. Red and blue glass are used at Rutlam, as well as at Pertabgurh, and the manufacture is in the hands of two or three families only. The processes are jealously guarded, and, if the few persons who know them were to die, the art would be lost. In this way many minor arts in India, and in the East generally, have been lost, and perhaps will never be rediscovered.

No. 269. A jade buckle set with gems. This is a small example of a purely oriental, perhaps characteristically Turanian art. Jade is extremely hard and is worked with difficulty, yet its beautifully soft colour forms such a charming foil for the richest gems that the jeweller in the East has ever loved to employ it. In the South Kensington Museum there is a splendid collection of vessels and ornaments worked in this precious stone and set with priceless gems. Amongst them was a bowl, upon which it is stated that no less than three generations of artists were engaged. In the Imperial Institute collection were several fine specimens that belonged to the great Lord Clive, the conqueror at Plassey. One of them, a *surahi* or goblet, was most choice. Jade handles have been much used for swords, daggers, bow rings, charms worn on the arm or suspended from the neck, inkstands, &c. In the Ulwar Treasury there is an exquisite box of perforated jade which is set with rubies and diamonds. The buckle is only a small specimen of the art, but is sufficient to illustrate the mode of using the material.

Nos. 273 and 274. Silver and gold spangles made in Jeypore and largely employed for ornamenting shoes.

Nos. 277 to 280. Gold and silver thread, also made in Jeypore, and used for many purposes such as shoemaking, embroidery, and brocades.

The case contains a good deal of silver jewellery.

No. 283. A *pachmaniya* or pendant and necklace of a Jeypore woman, made by a jeweller, at the time a prisoner in the Jeypore Jail, is pretty, and is a good example of fine workmanship. There are five balls representing the flowers of the jujube tree (*Zizyphus jujuba*), which are united by a tube of silver. This forms the necklace, and hanging from it is a plaque composed of a number of rhombs embossed with a dog tooth ornament and united together by links. This design is old.

Nos. 288 to 316. Small ornaments from Simla and Kulu. These are worn throughout North India, chiefly by Mohamedan women, and the females of the hill tribes, or of low castes of Hindus. Many of the designs are adaptations from floral patterns, such as buds or leaves.

Burmese jewellery is well represented ; the forehead ornaments (Nos. 234 and 327) of silver filigree. The latter made up in part of peacocks in their pride (the crest of Burmah), are used by Englishmen as necklaces. The beetle-shaped brooch (No. 318) is cleverly made.

No. 338 is the official water-ladle of the minister of a Burmese king. It was bought at Mandalay just after the conquest of Upper Burmah.

Nos. 340 and 341 are two silver jointed fish from Kharakpur, near Monghyr in Bengal. They form bottles for antimony or *surma*. The dark pigment or *kohl* is used in the East for painting on the margins of the eyelids, to add to the beauty of the eyes and to relieve them from the painful glare of the bright sunlight.

No. 325. A rare and choice silver embossed pipe for smoking tobacco; made in Japan. From the same country comes a sword 485 years old, with a small attached knife, with which it was the etiquette for the owner to make the first cut if his honour ever required that he should commit suicide or perform the *harikiri* ceremony on himself. Such was the custom in former days in Japan. The man was usually killed outright by his friends or servants. The handle of the sword is an exquisite example of the delicate manipulative skill and artistic treatment of metal by the Japanese artists.

Revolving frames on the marble pillar (No. 16).

These contain brocades from Benares, such as have already been described; gold lace from Trichinopoly and Benares; as well as some specimens of embroidery from different parts of India.

No. 351 is a long scarf or *mandil* from Burhanpur in the Central Provinces. This city was the seat of Government in that part of India in the days of the great Moghuls, and the governors or viceroys were not infrequently sons or near relatives of the emperors of Delhi. It was near the renowned fortress of Asirgarh, and through it ran the main road from the Deccan and the West Coast, along which the early travellers, as for example Sir T. Roe, passed to Agra and Delhi. As the seat of a large court, it became a sumptuary art centre, and the manufacture of gold lace, scarves, &c., is one of the industrial arts which has still clung to the place. Here too were recently found a good many fine specimens of old porcelain vases, which had belonged to wealthy nobles of the past, and were of course imported, as there is no trace of porcelain manufacture in India.

The specimens of lace for sword belts (Nos. 352-355) and some small handkerchiefs (No. 360) were presented by H. H. the Nizam of Hyderabad. Nos. 356 and 363 are brocades or *kincobs* from Ahmedabad. Fine pieces of this cloth of gold are still manufactured.

The patterns are smaller than those of Benares, and are even more disfigured by the use of aniline dyes.

WALL FRAMES NOS. 17, 18 AND 19.

No. 370 is a still more striking example of the disastrous effect of the use of the *naya rang*, the new colours or coal-tar dyes. It is a veil or *sari* from Poona. Granting that in experienced hands the employment of these pigments may be justified on the score of cheapness, there is not the slightest doubt that they have had deplorable results in ruining the beauty and value of many textile industries in the East. Nos. 371 and 372 are photographs of Burmese plate made in Rangoon for Mr. Strang Steel. This gentleman exhibited at the Imperial Institute some of the largest pieces of the kind, the above amongst them, which have been made in Burmah for Europeans. They will be referred to again in connection with the specimens in Case No. 44.

Recess Case No. 20.

This contains for the most part old metal-ware, which is chiefly of interest on account of its classical forms.

At the top of the case are two women's veils which are stamped in pure gold and silver. They are specimens of chintz manufactured at Sanganir, an old town 8 miles south of Jeypore. The chintzes or cotton fabrics which are made at this place enjoy a high reputation for the purity of their colours, durability of the material, and great variety of their designs, but they have had to suffer, not only from the aniline plague, but from the competition of the European dealers, whose chemists and commercial travellers have enabled their employers to turn out such exact machine-made imitations as to deceive the greatest native experts. For a time the European fabrics were too perfect, but a blurred roller or careless dab of pigment soon completed the resemblance to the hand-made articles, and ere long will drive them out of the field.

The patterns in the examples exhibited have been traced in the precious metals, and their delicate contrast with the green and yellow stuffs on which they are imprinted makes them very choice indeed.

Below the veils will be seen No. 376, a green shield with an enamelled border. It is made of the skin of the nilgao antelope, the blue cow, or *Rusa Aristotelis.*

No. 576, in case 38, is a similar shield with a red ground. In some cases the black tuft of hair, which is found on the dewlap of the animal, is left to project from the centre of the shield.

This art is confined to several persons in Ahmedabad, but the most skilful of them, Parshotam Das, made a wonderful specimen for H. R. H. the Duke of Connaught, which was exhibited at the Imperial Institute. It was perfectly transparent, and was carved in four panels as well as enamelled. Each panel represented one of the delicate stone windows of the mosque in the *bhadar* or old citadel of Ahmedabad. These windows, which are filled with tracery, are renowned throughout India. The figures are chiefly palms and other trees arranged in a singularly graceful fashion. Unless fortune is kind, here is another art which bids fair to disappear at no distant date.

The remaining shields in the case are commercial examples. A small shield, with a red patch in the centre, is still the official symbol of the *dhalait* or messenger of the State, but is no longer of use in war. Shields such as the above are made in Jeypore for the tourist, but the market is at present a little overstocked with them. Weapons of all kinds and shapes are also manufactured for the same purpose, and a few of the most interesting will be found in the different cases. The art of manufacturing antiquities is not unknown in Jeypore. No. 378 is a mace with a cow's head, *garshasp*, from Persia.

It was the royal symbol of authority of the ancient kings of that country, and in the Shahnamah, the famous epic of the Persian sovereigns, one reads how the royal line was in ancient times saved by a divine cow; hence the honour done to that animal.

No. 380. A zinc water bottle or *surahi.*

Before machine-made ice was in such universal use, it was customary to employ an *abdar* or waterman to cool water in zinc bottles of various forms by covering them with pit ice or freezing mixtures composed of various salts. The water vessels in this case are very instructive as regards the shapes in vogue amongst different castes and in different provinces of India. For example, No. 383 a water-bottle with oblique ribs on the neck and bowl, from Surat.

No. 388, the handsome *hastawa* or ewer of old Bidri work, with diaper floral ornament in gold, comes from Ujain, the ancient Hindu town in Malwa or Central India which was the capital of Vikramaditya in B.C. 56, from which time the ordinary Hindu or Sambut year is dated.

No. 390 is an ewer from Bombay with fluted bowl having, as motive for the design, the *kamrakho* or *averrhoa* fruit.

No. 398. A gourd-shaped waterpot or *kamandalu*, such as is used by the *bairagis* or religious mendicants in Bengal. This is made of brass inlaid with copper. The union of two metals in Indian art work is termed *Gunga-Jamni* in allusion to the meeting of the pure waters of the stream of the Jamna with the muddy current of the Ganges below the fort at Allahabad, at what is called the Triveni, strictly the *sangam* or union of three rivers: the third in this case is the mystic Saraswati from heaven, which is shewn trickling down in drops to water a sacred ficus or fig tree in an underground room in the fort to this day.

No. 397. A rosewater sprinkler or *gulab pashi* from Nasick, used chiefly by Mohamedans for sprinkling over guests at their departure or on the conclusion of a visit or festival.

No. 403. Ganges water vessel or *chambu*. For a lengthy description of these vessels the reader is referred to the description of the contents of case No. 323, Mythological Room No. 15.

FRAMES NOS. 21 TO 26.

No. 407. Cloth in which narrow strips of silver thread are interwoven in the stuff forming the textile termed *khes*, from Burhanpur.

Nos. 408 to 411. Pieces of black net embroidered in gold scrolls and beetle wings (the elytræ or wing cases of one of the Buprestidæ) from Trichinopoly, Madras Presidency. By way of contrast, a piece of dado cloth stamped with gold from Japan is shewn (No. 412).

RECESS CASE NO. 27.

This case contains a number of specimens of pierced, engraved, and chased brass from Ispahan in Persia, which are ornamented in many cases with medallions of quaint figures. The best pieces are Nos. 424, a vase, and 427, an incense-burner. The latter were used by ancient Persian fire-worshippers to perfume their bodies and houses as far back as the the time of Herodotus.

No. 432. Lamp stand.

No. 438. A large perforated camel, which may serve as a perfume-burner.

No. 441. A salver with borders of engraved and chased mythological figures.

No. 446. A fruit box of steel in the form of a duck.

CASE NO 28.

Here will be found larger and finer pieces of Ispahan work.

No. 453. This is a steel peacock with broad expanded tail 18½ inches wide, which is covered with chased and engraved figures representing a king surrounded by a court of demons *deo* or *jins* and female figures *pari*. The head and breast are gilt. The eyes are formed of rubies and turquoises, and the neck, thighs, and some other part of the bird are damascened in gold. The total height is 3 feet.

No. 457. A torch stand.

No. 458. A flattened box.

No. 459. A bowl.

No. 461. A bathroom lamp.

Nos. 463 to 468, 486 and 487, &c., are from Peshawar. The shapes are Afghan, and the material copper, which has been plated with tin, through which intricate arabesque designs have been cut down to the richer coloured ground.

Nos. 470 to 472. Articles made at Trichinopoly of mixed metal or zinc with brass incised ornament.

Nos. 473, 474, 478, 479, 489 and 490. These are specimens of Bidri work from Purneah (Parnia) in Bengal. They are similar to the Lucknow Bidri, but the designs are thought by Sir George Birdwood to be partly of Chinese origin, and the fish emblem is not represented.

Nos. 475, 480 and 481 are specimens of the same art from Murshidabad, also in Bengal.

Nos. 494, 498, 499, 500. Trays of embossed copper. A good deal of this work is manufactured for domestic purposes amongst Musalmans at Lucknow, the capital of Oudh.

At the back of the case is a large sunshade (No. 495), which was worked in 1886 in the girls' school at Jeypore. It is intended to be carried before a Chief in processions. On one side it is embroidered with the rayed sun in the midst of figures of Hindu deities, and on the other with the crescent moon surrounded by Krishna and the milkmaids representing the Rasamandala or motion of the heavenly sphere under the symbol of a dance. The Surajvansi or one great clan of Rajputs descend from the sun ; the Chandravansi from the moon. (See the Introductory Chapter, page 5.)

Case No. 30.

There will be found in this case a fine series of electrotypes in copper of Indian vessels by Messrs. Elkington & Co., which were presented in exchange by the Lords of the Council of Education of Great Britain and Ireland. The originals are in the South Kensington Museum.

No. 503 is a fine specimen of Japanese metal-work—a large bronze vase with beautiful floral ornament, and a bird in relief in gold, silver, and colour.

No. 530. A large salver made in Poona by Govind Vishwanath Dongre of ruddy copper. There is a broad border with ten incarnations of Vishnu in repoussé round a floral medallion in the centre.

No. 531. A brass salver, on which are painted designs with Aspinall's enamel pigments. These are made at Tilhar, near Shahjehanpur. Painted metal salvers distinctly violate one of the canons of art that the usefulness of the article ornamented should not be injured, and the employment of the commercial enamels, which are very suggestive of the crude aniline colours, is very undesirable. The Tilhar wood-work is far more artistic.

No. 532. The Pilgrim's Progress Shield. The original was a chef d'œuvre of Mons. Morel Ladeuil, who designed it for Messrs. Elkington & Co. It is shown here, as are other examples of ancient and modern European art in some of the other rooms, in order that Indian artizans and visitors may not only see what is elsewhere regarded as truly great art-work, but also that they, as well as students, may compare them with the products of Eastern lands.

Recess Case No. 31.

A collection of *hookahs* in the East is always interesting. The pipe, being a constant friend and companion of all classes, is an object of general attention, hence the desire to make it as handsome as possible. In this case will be found specimens of metal *hookahs* from different parts of India, such as plain ones of white metal, which are in much use in Rajputana, from Bhilwarra in Meywar on the south-west of the State (Nos. 538, 540 and 549).

No. 561. The *hookahs* and *chillams*, or fire receptacles of mixed metal, from Jhunjhunu in the north of Jeypore, are also in great demand.

The case contains some salvers of *koft* and *tahnishan,* true and false damascening, from Sialkot in the Punjab (Nos. 535, 536) and specimens of enamelled copper from Kashmir.

The brass lamp suspended by a long chain is such as is used in Hindu temples (No. 564).

Wall Frames Nos. 32 to 37.

The *lungis* or long waist and loin cloths in these frames come from Bahawalpore in the Punjab.

They are made of striped silk interwoven with gold and silver thread, and are usually worn by Mohamedans (No. 568). They average 12 feet 14 inches in length and 28½ in width.

Recess Case No. 38.

This case is principally devoted to Kashmir copperware of different kinds. The trays (Nos. 580 to 583 : 593 to 596), and such like articles of plain ruddy copper, are engraved with deep patterns having the shawl design for the most part as the motive. These pieces are sometimes electroplated in India and Europe, as for example Nos. 585 to 590, which were thus treated at the School of Art, Jeypore.

The more common practice is to plate them in the old-fashioned way with tin (Nos. 579, 584, 601 to 605, 608 to 612). In others a kind of black composition or niello is used. Other ware may more properly be spoken of as enamelled. The ground is brass, and the patterns are worked out in red and black colours. Examples are : No. 591, a waterpot ; No. 606, a teapot ; No. 613, a stand supporting flower vases shaped like cornucopiæ ; and No. 614, a biscuit box.

Wall Frames Nos. 39 and 40.

No. 623. A collection of silk trouser cords used by Punjab men and women.

Pillar Frame No. 42.

Pillar Frame No. 42. Nos. 625 to 661, 683 to 710. A large and varied selection of embroidered borders in gold and silver from Surat, with similar borders and lace (Nos. 664 to 682) from Delhi. There are also 50 specimens of gold and silver lace from Jeypore and 3 from Burhanpur. These may well be studied together for the variety, delicacy, and skill of the decorative designs employed. Burhanpur was, as already stated, long the seat of a Moghul viceroy's court.

Frame No. 41.

No. 624. These are photographs of the celebrated Celtic brooch which was found at Tara, the ancient capital of Ireland. It is now in the Museum of the Royal Irish Academy in Dublin; and dates from the 10th century A.D. The special reason for showing it here will be found in the plaited gold chain attached to it, the design of which will be seen in every bazar in Upper India. The Celts had skilful priests, who worked in the precious metal and may have learned their art from Byzantium or Constantinople. The goldsmiths of North India derived many of their designs from the Mohamedans, who learned much of what they knew from the same seat of Imperial Empire in the East. When the emperors of Constantinople were not fighting with the Arabs, who overran Syria and conquered Damascus, and sometimes even when their lieutenants were at war with them, they often helped or propitiated the Musalmans by enriching their mosques and private buildings, by giving them presents, or by sending them skilled artizans to decorate their furniture and weapons. So also when the seat of the Caliphate was moved from Damascus to Baghdad, artists of all kinds went with it to the court of Harun-al-Raschid, and still later Timur (Tamerlane) conquered the oldest city in the world, and dispersed its artizans through his vast dominions. These are but straws to indicate how the arts have been diffused, and to show how impossible it is to decide where any particular art originated.

We can see the influence in part, but cannot tell where the beginning arose. I myself found in a shop in Stambul a vase which had been specially made in Jeypore according to an old design furnished by me several years before. It had come through Central Asia, and was being sold as old Persian ware.

Case No. 43.

This case is principally devoted to the display of enamels from many Eastern countries, in order that they may be compared with specimens of Jeypore work, which are in the opposite cases. There are also a few examples of metal ware from Japan, &c.

Silver enamel.—No. 764, a pen-box from Lucknow, silver parcel gilt, champlevé enamel, or that in which the ground and edges of the design are formed by the plate itself.

Nos. 765, 781, two bowls, and No. 827, a salver from Lucknow, of the same kind, but enriched with bands of delicate flowers and animals. Both these specimens are of very fine workmanship, being well designed and finished. They are perhaps a little too much covered with ornament. The salver, 6⅝ inches in diameter, cost Rs. 42, and was made by Ajodhya Pershad.

705 COPPER EYE FOR AN IDOL. JEYPORE.
829 HAIR ORNAMENT. SILVER ENAMEL. MULTAN.
826 VASE. SILVER ENAMEL. BAHAWALPORE.
784 CUP WITH COVER. COPPER ENAMEL. ABKHORA, SRINAGAR, KASHMIR.
781 SMALL BOWL. SILVER ENAMEL. LUCKNOW.
10844 ENAMELLED CUP, &c. IRON. KASHGAR.
774 SALT CELLAR. SILVER ENAMEL. KASHMIR.
774A BOTTOM OF 774.
802 INKSTAND, SILVER ENAMEL. JEYPORE.
815 BUTTON. SILVER ENAMEL. MULTAN.
803 ENAMELLED IRON CRUTCH HANDLE. JEYPORE ARMOURY.

VII. ENAMEL ON GOLD, SILVER, COPPER AND IRON.

The Kangra enamel, Nos. 766, 767, 782, 833, 834, is of quite a different character, being coarse in design and colour, as also may be said of that which comes from Hydrabad in Sind (Nos. 783, 785 to 794), or from Delhi (Nos. 768 and 769).

The boldest examples in colour and design are No. 805, an antimony holder (*surmadani*) from Bahawalpur, and a vase or *abkhora* from the same place (erroneously marked as sold at Multan). In the latter piece numerous colours, especially orange and red, are introduced with good effect and considerable skill, as it is difficult to apply these hues to silver. The Multan enamel generally (buttons, Nos. 815 to 824 : necklaces, No. 828, and such like ornaments) is blue with occasionally light yellow on the plain silver ground. It gives one the idea of aniline rather than of rich metallic oxides.

Some specimens of silver enamel from Jeypore are also exhibited. The best of these is an inkstand in the form of a boat, which was made at the School of Art, but the Jeypore artist does not care to work on a less valuable substance than gold, alleging that the colours will not adhere to the baser metal. Close by it is the handle of a devotee's crutch, which is lent by H. H. the Maharaja of Jeypore from his private collection. It is of blue enamel on iron with floral encrustations in gold. The piece is unique, and proves that the base after all does not make much difference, although it is true certain colours can be applied to the king of metals alone.

The silver enamel from Kashmir is generally coloured a delicate light blue, and is much more pleasing than that from Multan (Nos. 724 and 725).

No. 776, a tumbler with the inside parcel gilt, has a beautiful vine leaf design in blue and green.

The copper ware, parcel gilt and enamelled, from Kashmir is much admired. There are some good specimens of it in the case, such as No. 784, the *abkhora* (or cup on a foot) of antique form. A *hookah*, No. 804, valued at Rs. 80 ; a coffee pot, No. 806, made by Subhana, of Srinagar, Kashmir ; a water-bottle or *surahi*, and three salvers, Nos. 836 to 838. Some of the examples, especially those made for, or by, Lassoo, coppersmith, of Srinagar, are not gilt, as for example the salvers Nos. 835 (A and B), and a box in the form of a Hindu temple. This is 9½ inches high, and cost Rs. 22.

At Jeypore copper is also enamelled, but, as the specimens Nos. 795 and 796, a pair of eyes for an image, will show, rather roughly.

Four common brass trays, with ornament in cloisonné enamel from Japan, show the different process in use in that country. The enamel is placed in compartments, or cloissons, which are formed by soldering strips of gold or other metal, which form the outlines of the design, to the ground or plate.

Here also will be found a few fine pieces of Japanese work, which prove how well those skilful people are acquainted with metallurgy in all its branches. No. 839 is a large salver of dark bronze with a water bird in silver, and lotuses in bronze, silver, and gold.

Nos. 845 and 846 are two old bronzes, the first being a figure subject, the second an incense-burner.

No. 799 is a water vessel of delicate cloisonné enamel, and No. 800 is a tea kettle of bronze with etched ornament in gold.

No. 777 is a tumbler in silver niello. Niello is a composition which is used in lieu of enamel, and work done in it is capable of showing much beauty. It is to enamel what a sketch in black lead pencil would be to a water-colour drawing. Lastly, there are several tea cups, saucers, and covers of enamelled iron from Kashgar in Turkestan. These are sold in the Peshawar bazar in large numbers.

As it has been generally admitted that enamelling on metal is a Turanian art, these specimens are of special interest, as they come from a country which links the remotest bounds of Upper and Eastern Asia to the South and West, or the Turanian to the Aryan lands.

SILVER CASE NO. 44.

This case contains specimens of silver ware from all parts of India. The two oldest specimens are electrotypes by Messrs. Elkington & Co. The first (No. 872), at the south end of the case, is a reproduction of the Bactrian salver of Dr. Lord, which was found in Kabul and deposited in the India Museum (now at South Kensington) in London. Upon it is represented the Triumph of Bacchus. It is of undoubted Greek origin, and illustrates, perhaps, the most dominant influence in early Indian art. The second example (No. 850) is a Buddhist relic casket, which was found in Kulu and is thought to be of not later date than the 12th century after Christ. The figures, that surround the cylinder, stand in niches, which may be either purely Buddhist or Byzantine. Garnets are introduced in two bands above and below the figures.

Jeypore is represented by specimens of different kinds, such as No. 847, a cream jug with engraved band round the margin and a handle formed like a snake which is being fed by Krishna, No. 851, a box supported on three crocodiles of embossed silver, with the figure of Ganesh, the Hindu god of wisdom, on the lid. These were made at the School of Art.

No. 858 is a *pan*-box of pierced brass, silver plated, with delicate flowers and birds, which are formed, in part, by the perforation and, in part, by the engravings. The maker was Raghunath of Jeypore. This kind of work was employed for *pan*-boxes, as the tracery allowed the *pan* or betel leaves to be exposed to the air, but it is now often used for soap boxes and even for larger articles, as for example the door of the Honorary Secretary's office in the Museum.

No. 848. A bowl which is enriched with delicate engraved scroll work by Pyari Lall of Ulwar. This man and other members of his family have attained some repute for the beautiful way in which they represent the fur and markings of animals by engraving.

Their plate is carefully finished, and shows the value of European influence when properly employed. They availed themselves of the instruction afforded at the School of Engineering at Roorki in the North-West Provinces.

No. 849. A drinking cup or tumbler, which is ornamented with chased figures of Rajputs in oval cartouches on a frosted ground, shows some such influence also. Here too the finish is good, but the Oriental cachet is retained in the figures. The maker works at Bikanir in the north-west of Rajputana, where, in the midst of the desert, live many rich bankers, who have earned their money, and still own shops in Hindustan. They, and the Chief of their Rajput State, have, by their liberal patronage, attracted artists of all kinds from all parts of India to the inaccessible and remote region in which they dwell. Many

203

10841

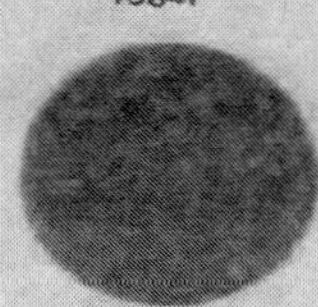

267

878

10845

870

10843

10841 GOLD MOHR. JEYPORE.
203 BOX, BIDRI WARE. HYDERABAD.
267 SILVER MEDAL. JEYPORE EXHIBITION, 1883.
10845 SILVER CRANE. MATHURA.

878 PARCEL GILT SILVER SALVER. JEYPORE.
10843 RUPEE. JEYPORE.
870 SILVER BOX. HIPPAWA, CEYLON.

XIII. BIDRI, SILVER AND COINS.

arts are therefore practised in these lands, for whose origin we must go to far-distant capitals.

No. 854. An *atrdan* or tray and bowl for *atr* of roses and the ingredients of *pan*, which are presented to guests when leaving the presence of their host.

This is an interesting piece of silver parcel gilt plate with a row of green glass beads round the edge of the stand. It was made at Bugru near Jeypore by Bal, a clever carpenter in the employ of the Chief.

Nos. 875, 877, 879, 881, Jeypore, and No. 878 from Indore. These are all silver salvers, for the most part with bands and centres of embossed floral ornament, which is parcel gilt. A good deal of plate of this kind is made at Seronge, a town and district in Central India which belongs to the Nawab of Tonk. Similar plate is, I believe, also made in Mysore, but most silversmiths in Rajputana seem to know how to manufacture it, and it is largely used by both Musulmans and Hindus: by the former for domestic vessels of all kinds which are usually parcel gilt and engraved and embossed; by the latter generally of plain silver only because the Hindu, for ceremonial reasons, uses rougher means of cleansing his food vessels. On the whole, it would seem that this special kind of work is of Mohamedan origin and perhaps took its rise in Central India or at the old courts of the Central Provinces.

Nos. 869, 876 and 877. A belt ornament of silver filigree with flowers in cloisonné enamel from Delhi.

No. 868. An *atrdan* of silver filigree, with enamel cover to the inside box, which contains compartments for *pan* and a small *kibalnuma* or compass to indicate to the Mohamedan owner the proper direction of Mecca, towards which he should always turn when praying.

The specimens of silver from Kashmir illustrate all the ordinary artistic methods of working in the metal which are in use in the Happy Valley. Subhana and Habibju are the principal dealers.

No. 852 is a sugar basin, of which the upper opening is in a plane cut at an oblique angle with the horizon. This *kang* shape is peculiarly high Asian, yet I observe that European dealers have recently given it to silversmiths in Cutch and Trichinopoly to ornament in their own special styles of surface decoration. It is in this way that confusion arises as to the origin of different styles, to say nothing of the utterly inartistic results when the articles are completed. Quite recently I saw three sugar basins of this shape on a lady's dining-room table all supplied by one firm, and all of them differently ornamented as above described.

It is unfortunately nearly always true that, as soon as Indian art ware becomes commercial, it is debased in form, design, and in every feature that makes it so interesting to the connoisseur.

A wide-mouthed vase of Japanese shape, which has been covered with repoussè floral ornament in Cutch, is another illustration of the evils of modern trade direction.

No. 861. As regards the Cutch ornament itself, Sir G. Birdwood holds that it is of Dutch origin, but that it is perfectly assimilated to the style of the province.

Nos. 853, 856 and 855. The two former, *viz.*, a cup on a pedestal of engraved silver, and an *abkhora*, also a drinking cup, both parcel gilt, and the last a gourd-shaped vessel with diaper ornament, are excellent specimens, in good taste, of Subhana's work.

No. 857. Another gourd-shaped vessel. The ornament is of the cone or cypress pattern, of which the origin has been variously described as from ancient Assyria or modern Persia.

The large water bottle or *surahi* (No. 859), the claret jug with snake handle and cone-pattern in arabesque medallions (No. 873), and the wine flagon with foliage, snakes, and birds on a minutely engraved ground, the whole in a dead white colour (No. 874), may be instructively examined and compared. They are characteristic specimens of Srinagar work. The snake is introduced very freely into Kashmir art. There are myths and traditions which relate to the former rule of the country by the Takshaka race or the Nagas of snake descent, or those races which, in all probability, had the serpent for their totem or symbol.

We now come to Burmah. No. 864, a large bowl in silver repoussé. A series of figures in high relief in niches in the midst of foliage surrounds the bowl. The artist was Moung Chivet Nee of Rangoon. He also made the flagon No. 866, in which the stem is formed of a female figure, and the cup of two bowls, the inner of which is smooth. The outer surface is pierced into figures in relief. These are good illustrations of work which is much admired " by connoisseurs all over the world," and which, according to Mr. Tilly, under the guidance of Europeans, is being much improved, while the national characteristics are zealously preserved. " He adds that the work is hammered, embossed, chased, and carved, and sometimes cut in open tracery, but is all made in exactly the same way."

The Burman artist treats silver in the right method, obtaining the greatest effect that the nature of the material allows. " Mr. Kipling also considers that the Burmese plate affords most valuable suggestions for the right treatment of silver," and now that silver has almost attained the position of a base metal, it may be anticipated that it will be more largely used for domestic purposes, especially as in England there is no longer a duty upon it, although the practice of hall-marking tells greatly against the popularization of Oriental plate in that country. A number of bowls, jugs, &c., and numerous photographs will be found in other parts of the Museum.

We can now turn to the plate, which is made at Kandi, in Ceylon, in which the metal is also treated with boldness.

Nos. 865, 867, 870 and 871. These are boxes or *hippawas.* No. 865 is oval, Nos. 867 and 871 are oblong with rounded ends, while No. 870 is of a peculiar curved form, with the ends terminating in the heads of dragons. Figures are represented in the midst of scroll-like foliage, and on the bottoms of the boxes are chased figures of animals and flowers. Two lessons are taught by these articles. First, the care, so characteristic also of Japanese and mediæval European work, with which every part, whether seen or unseen, is equally faithfully and honestly dealt with. Secondly, the dangers of excess of ornament; here, however, somewhat less inappropriate than usual, owing to the smallness of the specimens.

The salvers Nos. 883, 884 and spoons, like the Apostle spoons of Europe, and Nos. 886 to 888, all from Kandi, should also be studied. The four raised swans with inter-twined bills of No. 883 suggest a Buddhist motive, as might be expected in the Buddhist artists of Ceylon, though the demons and sun of No. 884 may indicate some recollection of their enemies, the Brahmanical conquerors of the island of Lanka or Ceylon in the age of the Ramayan, the great Hindu epic poem which is still so well known throughout India. In front of the case is a fine *atrdan* of silver filigree from Cuttack in Bengal (No. 882). It is

1023 VASE WITH GROOVED BOWL.
1022 ROSEWATER SPRINKLER.
2250 VASE.

2247 ROSEWATER SPRINKLER.
986 RUSSIAN CENSER.
973 CHUSKI, VESSEL FOR DRINKING SPIRIT.

1020 ROSE WATER SPRINKLER
1000 VASE
2396 CHUSKI OR DRINKING VESSEL.

X. BRASS WARE FROM JEYPORE.

very similar to the Maltese silver work or to that of the Ionian Islands. In the Indian Metal Work Exhibition in London some fine specimens of this kind in gold, which belonged to the first Lord Clive, were exhibited. As the Cuttack work is nearly all European in shape, I am inclined to think that this art may have been introduced into Cuttack, Dacca, and Murshidabad from Europe, perhaps early in the last century.

Revolving Frames on Pillar and No. 45.

Nos. 888 to 890 : 896 to 903. Two hundred and ten specimens of gold and silver lace from Jeypore, all of different patterns. The trade in these fabrics was formerly very large, but chiefly in pure metal, as there was a heavy fine for making false lace. The latter is now, however, in great demand for marriage and other purposes. A royal lady's dress or skirt may contain as much as 40 pounds' weight of gold trimming.

Nos. 892 to 895. Four groups of peacocks' feathers with eyes embroidered in gold. These are used in making *morchals* or state plumes or fly whisks, which are held by the attendants behind a prince. The custom is one which rose out of necessity, and is very ancient, as may be judged from Egyptian and Assyrian paintings and sculptures. The great facility of surface decorative power possessed by the Indian artist is clearly shown in these groups of lace and embroidered feathers.

Niche Case No. 49.

Nos. 909 to 934 : 941 to 942 : 945 and 949 to 952 (wall frame). These are all pieces of the well-known engraved brass from Benares. This manufacture has much deteriorated on account of the demand in large quantities for cheap specimens. Old examples are interesting. The salvers being raised towards the centre are not of much use, though they are perhaps more effective than if flat.

The practical advantages of having a flat surface are, however, well seen in the case of the Jeypore salvers, for which there is, for that very reason, a steadily increasing demand.

Nos. 935, 936, 943, 947. Lucknow embossed brass and copper. There is a large trade in these articles at Lucknow, the capital of Oudh, as well as for similar work at Jhansi (Nos. 938 to 944) in the North-Western Provinces.

Wall Frames Nos. 52 and 55.

These contain *mandils* or turbans of cloth with stripes of gold thread from Burhanpur.

Wall Frame No. 53, and Nos. 948 to 951.

The scrolls show the Japanese mode of using gold thread in embroidery.

Recess Case No. 56.

(Jeypore Brass.)

This recess case, and the large case, No. 57, contain a collection of Jeypore brass-ware. Before describing the contents of the case, the following extracts from other works of mine seem necessary. I have modified them only to indicate where examples quoted may be found in the Jeypore Museum.

It will be at once apparent that for the Hindu (I use the word in this place to indicate religion, not race) religion, as expressed by symbolism and by mythology generally, is the keystone to his art.

This then is the motive which prevails throughout Jeypore work, and, in order to fully understand it, the collection of marble images, in which all the ordinary forms of the gods are represented (Case No. 309, Stone Room), and of metal figures, and the apparatus used in religious worship or *puja* (Cases Nos. 323 and 324, Mythological Room), should be carefully studied. Jeypore supplies all Brahmanical India with its stone images, in which, after consecration alone, is the deity, or a portion of his spirit, supposed to reside. In the marble set of figures, great care has been taken to give the different figures their proper symbols, colours, &c. There is, however, in Jeypore another art motive. There was a close alliance between the rulers of the State and the great Moghul emperors of Delhi, for whom indeed they often acted as viceroys in distant provinces. This connection accounts, not only for the Mohamedan influence in Indian art of a powerful central authority and court, but also explains why the arts of Persia and Central Asia, or even of Burmah and China, should have somewhat reacted on the work of the subjects of a Jeypore prince, who at one time was Governor of Kabul and at another conquered, for the Paramount Lord, the Province of Orissa on the East of Hindustan, and also ruled Bengal and made Assam tributary. Early traces, moreover, of European influence would be specially felt at Jeypore, but particular attention must be drawn to the effect which the severe taste of the Mohamedan court has had upon the Jeypore school. Abundant evidence of it will be seen in the cases in the forms of vessels, in the arabesque designs of the salvers, and in the absence, as a rule, in such articles, of representations of the human form.

This is more observable in work of Musalman Indian inspiration, as the Indian is a Sunnite ; while the Persian, who has so much modified art in the country, is a Sheeah, with far less strict notions on the subject.

From these remarks it is also abundantly clear that the local artist has never been free to follow one school, but has naturally been swayed by that which was most dominant or most fashionable at the moment. The actual workman has generally been a Hindu, who has possessed infinite patience and great mechanical skill, born of long practice and hereditary aptitude. He has been a man of very imitative tendencies, who has been ever ready to follow the lead of the stronger mind, or the most powerful fashion of the time.

The tools used in making the brass-ware are of primitive character. Specimens of them, as well as clay models showing the artists at work, will be found in the room behind the east gallery upstairs. In Case No. 118 also will be seen, in different stages of manufacture, a set of brass trays with ornament in repoussé showing how that class of work is made.

The brass is first formed into the shape of a tray, and then cleaned and coated with white chalk or paint upon which the outlines of the design are drawn and engraved. The surface is next covered with a thick layer of pitch, and the design is brought up into high relief by hammering. It is afterwards chased, engraved, and polished. A number of these salvers will be found in the cases and on the walls in the metal rooms Nos. 2 and 3.

Nos. 2439 to 2446 in Case No. 118 show the whole process of manufacture.

Nos. 956, 958, 968, 974, 979 and 985. These are small round 10-inch trays, which were embossed and engraved with patterns taken from the soffits of the arches of the tomb of Khan Khanan at Delhi. A chased peacock fills up the centre of No. 968.

No. 757. This tray is 18 inches in diameter. Its edge is scalloped, and the arabesque design comes from Humayun's tomb at Delhi.

The following are the principal specimens in the case :—

No. 961. An ewer with lobed body and engraved ornament, 12 inches high, from Jeypore. Cost Rs. 15.

No. 962. A rolling lamp of perforated brass, originally made at Duni in Jeypore, but copied at many other places. The light is suspended in the centre of several skeleton globes which are arranged within each other on the principle of a ship's compass.

No. 964. Water Jug. Pattern taken from the Kamrakh or Averrhoa Carambola fruit.

No. 965. A small cup with a tiny spout. The *chuski*, literally the sipping or sucking vessel, which is used by the Rajput for drinking strong liquors. He moistens the tip of his tongue with a drop or two of strong alcohol, and thus keeps up constant excitement, so that he imbibes an immense quantity of spirit in the course of the day without being offensively intoxicated. It is the most pernicious form of drinking.

No. 967. A *kamandalu* or gourd-shaped waterpot with handle. It is covered with engraved mythological figures. It is a Bengal shape, and is used by devotees.

No. 969. Bowl for holding hot ashes (*agdan*). It is supported by a figure of Garuda, the Vulture King and the vehicle of Vishnu.

No. 970. Water bottle or *surahi*. The pattern is adopted from No. 972, which was copied from a painting in the Emperor Akbar's Razmnamah. It is made up of portions of animals, and is embossed with grotesque figures in the midst of raised foliage.

No. 975. Coffee pot, Bokhara form. The centre of the bowl is set with garnets. The whole surface is covered with engraved figures. Strictly these ought to have been Jins or fairies, and not representations of Hindu gods, as the shape is decidedly Mohamedan.

Nos. 977, 978, 986. Three censors. The first is Russian ; the third was copied in Jeypore from it, and is more highly finished ; the second was reproduced from the drawing of a more elaborate Russian original, which is now at South Kensington. It is of brass with silver-plated raised ornament. Byzantine or Byzanto-Russian pieces of metal ware are well suited for reproduction in Jeypore.

No. 984. A fine water vessel, with two handles and embossed floral ornament, the shape of which also comes from the Razmnamah.

No. 987. Water bucket or *dol*, brass, covered with engraved figures. Iron vessels of this shape are used for drawing water from wells.

CASE NO. 57.

This case is also filled with Jeypore work.

No. 989. A large vase 20½ inches high, globular with a flat lid, on which is seated Ravana, the Demon King of Ceylon, armed with a great number of weapons. The bowl is enriched with panels which show in repoussé scenes from the Ramayana, the most ancient of the great epic poems of India.

No. 991. A large Ganges water-vessel made at the School of Art, Jeypore. Engraved with mythological designs. The original came from Benares.

No. 993. Model of a kiosk or *chhatri*, such as is placed as a cenotaph over the spot on which the body of a Rajput hero or noble is burned. At the *mahasati* or cemetery at Udaipur I counted 22 figures on one *sati* stone. At Bundi I believe as many as 60 or 70 may be found, and in several cases there are representations of men, who also terminated their existence by voluntary cremation with their lord. At Udaipur there is a specially interesting cenotaph before the greater building erected in honour of Maharana Amar Singh. It is in memory of a sweeper who immolated himself. This is pointed out as a worthy example of devoted service. Beneath the dome of the stone kiosk stands a slab, on which is engraved an armed man with figures before him of as many wives as have burned themselves on the funeral pyre. Above them the sun and moon are carved as witnesses for ever of the great deed.

No. 998. Cock-shaped engraved water-vessel.

No. 1000. A small vase with handles in the form of lizards climbing up the sides. Used for ink or antimony. Copied from a Nepalese vase.

No. 1001. A vase with grooved bowl and two parrots near the neck. Reproduction of a Jain vessel.

No. 1003. An elephant goad or *ankush*. Iron, engraved, and pierced. From the School of Art, Jeypore. The making of such goads is rather a speciality of Udaipur, where they are usually presented by the Chief to high officials on their departure from his court.

No. 1004. Water-vessel with snake-shaped handle.

Nos. 1008, 1009, 1011, 1013 and 1014. Betel boxes of different forms. Perforated and engraved. For a full description see No. 858 in the silver case (No. 44).

No. 1021. This is a bowl of elegant form. It is generally supposed to be Indian, but is really copied from a fine salt cellar designed by Benvenuto Cellini, the great Italian master.

Nos. 1020, 1022. Two rose water sprinklers of good form.

No. 1024. A salver engraved with figures of Krishna and the Gopis, or cowherdesses, dancing the mystic dance, in which the former multiplied himself, so that each woman imagined she had the true Krishna beside her. It is sometimes known as the *Rasmandala*, or dance to imitate the motion of the planets in the celestial vault.

No. 1027. A fine salver with a single female figure standing between two trees. Taken from a stone carving on the cenotaph of Maharaja Sawai Jai Singh, the founder of Jeypore, which is at Gehtore, a village near the town of Jeypore.

Nos. 1028 to 1032. Small well-made figures of animals in brass. Average height 1¼ inch, and cost Re. 1-8.

Nos. 1038 and 1043. Two maces, of which the first ends in a tiger's head ; used by the State *chobdars* or head peons as symbols of office.

No. 1046. Salver. The design is taken from a fine old Moradabad tray.

No. 1047. A large oval tray 30 inches by 22 inches. Engraved with an elaborate design, showing a tiger hunt. The artist worked for the School of Art, Jeypore, but was trained at Roorki.

Nos. 1048, 1052, 1054, 1059. Four silver-plated copper poles used as supports for the canopy or cloth of estate, which covers a royal seat or throne, forming a *shamiana.* Engraved and embossed with diaper patterns.

Nos. 1049, 1058. Brass shields, embossed with floral ornament in arabesques and also natural flowers and bosses, which are formed like the heads of the sun god or lions.

Nos. 1050, 1055. Salvers with designs from Batashawala's tomb, Delhi.

No. 1053. Salver from the tomb of Nadir.

No. 1057. A very fine salver. In the centre are two *apsaras* or heavenly nymphs, one of them pouring wine into a cup held by the other. Taken from the cenotaph of Maharaja Sawai Jai Singh.

No. 1060. An Emu's egg embroidered with *salma*, or gold thread, and pearls by Rahim Baksh, Zardoz, an Ulwar man. The design is formed by sewing the threads and beads through the hard shell.

No. 1061. A large brass salver, 30 inches in diameter, which is suspended in a frame above the entrance door of the room. There is another of different design over the opposite door.

No. 1064. Circular Burmese Gong. Mounted on a teak-wood stand.

Nos. 1065 to 1070. Burmese Gongs. Triangular. These are suspended from the bottom of the enamel Case No. 43, and close to them is a large Turkish Mangala or fire brazier, such as is used in the shops and houses of Stamboul or the Turkish quarter of Constantinople.

No. 1071. A suit of Japanese armour. Mounted on a dummy.

No. 1072. The coat of chain mail, trousers, and steel helmet of a Rajput. Mounted on a dummy.

CHAPTER III.

METAL ROOM No. II.

This is the room on the north side of the chief metal room.

Round the greater part of this room, and the one next to it, as well as the adjacent cross corridor, will be found a series of frames which contain jewellery in base metal. In former times women of the lowest castes were not allowed to wear gold and silver ornaments; others from choice did not do so. The upper classes, who use jewellery made of the precious metals and gems, value both chiefly for their intrinsic worth, and, in times of family trouble or general scarcity, sell or break them up, and, when prosperous again, of course have them re-made in the newest fashion. It is not so with base metal, which was never worth remelting, in consequence of which such ornaments are often of very archaic form, and, amongst the Banjaras and other wandering tribes, they often descend through several generations of women. The antiquity of many of the forms may be at once recognized by comparing them with the ornaments which are carved on the old Buddhist and Brahmanical images in the courts of the Museum.

The student will thus be able to note the origin of many of the modern types, the buds of flowers, the old Jain, or Buddhist, bell design, the different kinds of dice, cubes, and other geometrical forms, and the imitations or derivatives from grasses, seeds, shells, and other natural objects. He will also trace the various influences of race, religions, and commerce. In short, in the story of peasant jewellery, the history of the country, of its inhabitants, and of their customs, will be laid as an open book before him. A work on the jewellery of India, with all that it suggests under these heads, as well as its relations to art and design, would be of immense interest. Numerous scattered papers on the subject will be found in the journal of Indian art and elsewhere, but a connected work is a desideratum. Our collection is chiefly devoted to North India, and is comparatively small. A complete series from all India would extend to several thousand specimens. The collection begins with the head and neck, proceeds onwards to the extremities, and ends with the toes. It is unnecessary to describe it here in detail. A few observations may, however, be of use.

FRAME No. 59.

No. 1078. Nose ring, *nath*. The large ring is only worn by married women.

No. 1092. Ear pendants, fish-shaped.

The fish decoration (part of the Mahi-Maratib) which was given by the emperors to great nobles, was especially esteemed in Oudh; hence in Lucknow it was the popular form for jewellery and for the decoration of buildings. It may also have a symbolic meaning as the emblem of fecundity.

No. 1095. Forehead ornament, *band*. A flat disc fixed by gum, &c., to the space between the eyes. Worn by women of all classes. Small birds, such as parrots and amatavats (*Fringilla amandava*), are taught to fly down and take this ornament from the foreheads of the women.

Nos. 1135 to 1138. Ear-rings in the shape of leaves of the Pipal tree (*Ficus religiosa*). The first ornament, a fig tree leaf, of which we have any record, was worn by Eve, and so

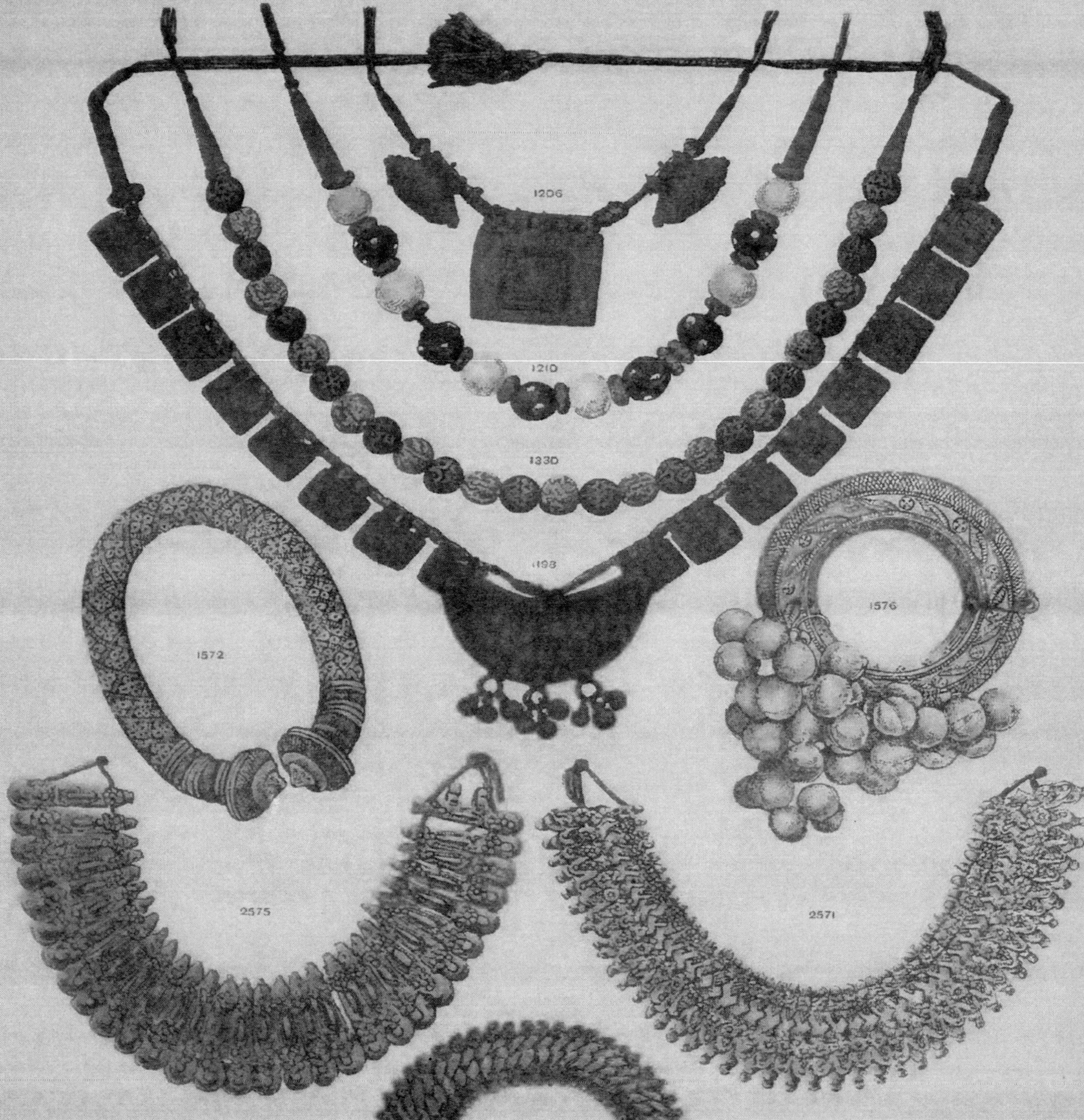

1206 CHARM. TAWIZ KA KATHLA, WORN BY YOUNG CHILDREN AND GIRLS.
1210 NECKLACE OF PEARLS AND STONES, WORN BY WOMEN IN RAJPUTANA.
1330 RUDRAKSH AND GOLD NECKLACE, WORN BY MEN IN RAJPUTANA.
1198 NECKLACE OF CHARMS, KATHLA, WORN BY WOMEN.

1576 FOOT ORNAMENT, WORN BY GUZERATI WOMEN.
3080 ANKLET, JEYPORE.
2575 ANKLET. NORTH-WEST PROVINCES.
2571 ANKLET. NORTH-WEST PROVINCES.
1572 KARA ANKLET, NORTH-WEST PROVINCES.

XVI. JEWELLERY (PEASANT).

wild tribes still make aprons of fig leaves in India. The ear is more distorted than any other human feature. Huge holes are made in the lobe to receive gigantic ornaments, and the cartilages are often pierced at short distances all round for the suspension of jewels. Not satisfied with this, bells and heavy objects are partially suspended by chains, which are fastened to the hair and hang across the forehead.

Nos. 1145 to 1154. Ten such rings are worn in one ear. The sect of Naths, or split-ear ascetics, who worship Shiva in Marwar, wear in the ear large flat circular glass rings 2½ inches in diameter.

FRAME NO. 60.

Nos. 1187 to 1208 are chiefly gilt necklaces and charms worn on the upper arm.

FRAME NO. 61.

The necklaces in this case (Nos. 1209 to 1235) are mostly set with imitation stones, the demand for which is very great in India, and is met partly from the country, but chiefly from Europe.

FRAMES NOS. 62 AND 63.

Nos. 1236 to 1297. Here most of the necklaces are made of glass beads, which are threaded with considerable taste and ingenuity in almost every conceivable geometric design.

FRAME NO. 64.

This case contains armlets and necklaces of grasses and seeds.

FRAME NO. 65.

Here also will be found rude necklaces of *jangal* or forest grasses, of tinsel, and even of wooden beads.

FRAME NO. 66.

Necklaces of which the beads are chiefly imitations of the buds of a flower, for example No. 1406, the Champa (*Michelia champaca*).

FRAME NO. 67.

Here are numerous specimens of bead necklaces, which are worn by women of all castes, and three reed pens that are also ornamented with glass beads.

OLD METAL CASE NO. 68.

In this case most of the exhibits have been selected for special reasons.

In the first place, for their forms, which are often very ancient ; in the second, on account of the great variety of surface ornamentation. It will be observed that objects, which are intended even for the most insignificant and trivial purposes, are enriched in this manner. The designs are simple, but are of endless variety, and of extreme interest from an historical point of view. Here one can trace the influences of many nations and periods. The love of external decoration does not imply great artistic power. It is a very early form of art. The savage loves to tattoo, or paint his person, or to cover his possessions with ornament, and, in thus adorning himself and his goods, happily fills up many hours which would otherwise be very wearisome.

It is moreover not very difficult, nor very intellectual, to go on reproducing, or even inventing, geometrical forms, but it is curious how certain designs repeat themselves in different lands, and amongst people who are very remote from each other. As regards shapes, many are derived from natural objects, others are symbolic, and, for the most part, these latter are the work of Hindu craftsmen. Many a vessel too suggests the influence of far-off lands, which, in the East, are after all not so very remote from each other, as pilgrims, from time immemorial, have served to link the most distant parts of Asia and Africa.

I will briefly allude to the objects of chief interest.

Nos. 1465 and 1467. Lamps with branches. In the former the principal oil receptacles are surmounted by cocks with long combs. The branches of the latter are imitated from some shrub.

Nos. 1466 to 1469. These are candle-sticks with semi-circular incurved supports for the lights, the whole springing from a pedestal which stands on a large tray. As a rule, in India, lamps of all kinds have a very wide circular tray at the base to keep them firm as well as to receive drippings of oil or fat.

No. 1468 is a hollow brass elephant, nearly a foot in height. It is curious that this animal is always fairly correctly represented, whereas every other beast is exaggerated and unnatural. His peculiarities are usually accurately seized, perhaps because there is an element of grotesqueness in the beast, that appeals to the uneducated Hindu mind, which always tends to magnify and exaggerate.

The case contains a number of toilet boxes, as for example No. 1470, a small specimen used to hold *roli* or a red powder of sandal wood and grains of rice, which is used by the heads of families or by priests to make the *tika* or forehead mark on auspicious occasions. The lid of the box is kept in place by a peacock-headed screw. The screw in India turns in the reverse direction to that in Europe. Although very few men are left handed, many things are done, in what Europeans would term the reverse way, in the East. The box is rudely ornamented with spots of red and green lacquer.

No. 1472 is in the shape of a mango, and is intended to contain offerings which are presented to a god.

No. 1480. Toilet box used by Mahratta women. There are five mango-shaped compartments, which are kept in place by a single peacock-headed screw. The following articles are usually put in it:—Sandal paste, rice, and spangles of gold or tinsel.

No. 1482. A box for betel leaves (*Piper chavica*).

No. 1483. A brass toy, an elephant on wheels. Toys of this kind are sold in large numbers in Indian bazars. The next few figures are chiefly from Vizagapatam. Sir G. Birdwood writes of a fine set, which belonged to H. R. H. the Prince of Wales, as follows:—"For the skilful modelling, finish, and a certain irresistible grotesqueness of expression these are the finest that I have ever seen. They graphically illustrate the whole gamut of military swagger in man and beast."

Mr. Carmichael, who lent a set to the Imperial Institute Exhibition of 1892, stated that the originals, some of which were in his possession, were reputed to have been made for a prince who had been directed to manœuvre his troops, in the hope that the necessary exercise would improve his health. In a truly Oriental way he preferred to have regiments of small brazen soldiers manipulated before him, thus obeying the letter, though not the spirit, of the orders of his physicians.

The grotesque imagination of the Burmese artist is well seen in the figures of the devils, Nos. 1491 and 1492.

No. 1495 is a small mango-shaped bottle for holding *surma* or antimony.

Nos. 1497 to 1503. Knives (*sarota*) for cutting the hard betelnut, Areca Catechu, or *supari*, one of the ingredients of *pan-supari*, the others being *chunam* (lime), catechu (*katha*), cardamoms (*elaichi*), cloves (*laung*), the whole wrapped up in a betel leaf. Some add *dhania* (coriander) seeds, mace (*jawatri*), cinnamon (*dalchini*), and even almonds (*badam*). On ceremonial occasions the leaves are covered with silver or gold leaf. The betelnut-cutter *sarota* (No. 1500) is highly ornamental.

Nos. 1505 and 1515. Two cups said to be made of quicksilver, but really of an alloy.

Nos. 1519 and 1520. Two brass *hookahs*. As is the case in Europe, so in India, there are many different arrangements for smoking tobacco. The poor man has a simple *chillam* or fire receptacle of clay, while his closed hands serve as a pipe stem, but, as a rule, the apparatus is composed of the *chillam* for the fire and tobacco, which are separated by a *tikri* or small piece of clay, the stem and mouthpiece ; and at the bottom, the *kali* or bowl, which is filled with water. The smoke passes downwards through the water, and is drawn up again into the mouth of the smoker. In the more elaborate specimens, a long tube or *nalcha*, or snake-like tube, intervenes between the bowl and mouthpiece.

No. 1522. Syringe with rose point. It is used at the festival of the Holi for throwing coloured water over a man's friends. Some of these syringes are very ornate and curious.

No. 1528. Globular brass box, with incised ornament, to contain the lime used by tobacco-eaters and as an ingredient for *pan*. Eating *zarda* or coarse tobacco is common amongst both Mohamedans and Hindus. It is held to be a bad, but not a disgraceful habit.

Nos. 1543 and 1546. Brass skin scratchers. A short time ago a patent was taken out for skin scratchers of porcelain or stone for use after the bath. The inventor observed that he had taken the hint from the remains of such articles which had been left by the ancient cave men. Skin scratchers have been always used in India, and are to this day employed by Hindus, especially for cleansing the soles of the feet after the bath.

No. 1551. A brass ink pot which can be suspended by cords ; it is used in Central India by seths or bankers. The Kayastha or clerk, and the serishtadar, the Musalman secretary or munshi, carry the implements for writing in an oblong box, which contains not only ink, but the reeds used as pens, scissors, and other small articles.

No. 1555. Back-scratcher in the form of a hand which is placed at the end of a long stick. In the last century fashionable people used such articles in Europe. There is one of enamelled gold in the Treasury at Ulwar, and pretty specimens in white and black ivory are made at Bahawalpur in the Punjab.

No. 1559. Handle of a walking stick which terminates in the head of an animal.

Nos. 1560 to 1565. Brass stirrups. These illustrate the desire for surface decoration, and the application of ornament to the most common articles. The spittoon (No. 2000) shows the same tendency.

No. 1571. Brass lizard from Trichinopoly. One of those curious examples of the Hindu fancy for producing something odd and strange.

Nos. 1572 to 1591, 1623 to 1635. Most of these articles are specimens of ornaments in base metal, such as are worn by women of low caste, and chiefly on the ankles.

No. 1574 is a huge shackle of mixed metal, which was heavy and sharp enough to ruin the gait, if not the ankles, of the unfortunate Gujerati woman who wore it. Some of the surface designs are elaborate. Most of the bangles are cast, but some, as for example Nos. 1579 and 1583, are formed of twisted wire.

Some of the early travellers in India refer to the women among the Rajputs as being enslaved early because they wore heavy shackles round their ankles.

Nos. 1623 to 1625. These are massive bands of metal which are worn by women of the Regar and other Hindu low castes. It is singular how inartistic some of the specimens are; in fact, provided there is some kind of ornament, the quality of it seems immaterial.

Nos. 1630 to 1632. *Bank* or W-shaped brass anklets worn by Bhil women, who, although their foot ornaments often weigh several pounds, yet cheerfully march many miles every day, carrying grass or wood on their heads. Old maids amongst Bheels are not rare.

No. 1603. Sandals or clogs of metal, which are used after bathing during religious worship to avoid the contact of leather, or for fear that the wet foot may be contaminated by something impure.

Nos. 1616, 1617. Antimony holders or flasks in the shape of a fish.

No. 1636. A dome-shaped betel box, which is pierced into an elaborated floral design.

No. 1638. A *chillam* or fire bowl of a *hookah*. Beside it (No. 1688) is a large *hookah*-base of mixed metal of zinc and brass with copper bands.

No. 1642. Water bottle of zinc. Such bottles are used because the water in them can be kept easily cool by freezing mixtures or by evaporation (No. 3100), Brass fish with a crescent on the back. It is fastened to the top of a pole and represents part of the Mahi Maratib or Fish Insignia, which was awarded to great nobles by the Delhi emperors. The actual insignia was composed of the gold head of a fish and two large balls. It was a most coveted distinction. It is the special cognizance of the Lucknow nawabs (afterwards kings of Oudh), and was also given to the Jeypore Maharaja by the Emperor Ferokhsher, and so great was the honour deemed that the musicians played three days and nights consecutively, and the whole city was given up to rejoicing when the news of the grant arrived.

No. 1672. A very handsome chain of rings, which is used as part of the trappings of cart bullocks.

No. 1683. A vessel for Ganges water (*Gangajali*) ornamented with a pretty scroll pattern. I procured a number of these vessels at Didwana in Marwar, an emporium of the salt trade.

FRAME NO. 69.

This contains arm and hand ornaments.

No. 1689. A *kara* or bracelet of twisted cords, which end in *bolas* or plum-shaped knobs. In No. 1690, the same ornament has the heads of two *magars* or crocodiles at the ends.

No. 1702. An ornament for the wrist or ankles ; it was cast in one piece. *Maraithi*.

Nos. 1704 and 1706. Bracelet of shell-like pieces threaded on silk or cotton. *Pahunchi.*

No. 1715. Armlet. *Bazuband.* Three imitation flat gems strung on with silk and gold wire cords.

Nos. 1722 to 1744. Rings of very varied forms.

FRAME NO. 70. *Also contains arm ornaments.*

No. 1759. Massive pieces or beads of mixed metal threaded on silk.

Nos. 1776 and 1777. Thin copper bracelets worn by Jogis or Shivaite ascetics. They are flattened bands covered with embossed figures of the god Mahadeo or his emblems, and from one side of each projects his principal symbol, the *ling*, with his bull, or Nandi, in front, and Parvati, his Shakti or wife, behind. Some are narrow, others wide. They are worn as *lingayat* bracelets.

No. 1790. A rude brass bracelet with pyramidal projecting bosses.

FRAME NO. 71.

Contains bracelets chiefly of zinc ; for example No. 1821. Formed of split bell-like pieces.

Nos. 1827 and 1829. *Pahunchis* or wristlets of bullet-like pieces.

FRAME NO. 72.

This frame is filled with bracelets and anklets, of which the most peculiar are Nos. 1846 and 1907, flattened anklets with ray-like ornaments ; they are usually worn by women of the *gujar* or shepherd class.

No. 1889. Composed of separate shell-like heart-shaped pieces.

No. 1906. Ring with depression for a piece of mirror glass.

FRAME NO. 73.

This frame is also filled with bracelets and anklets.

Nos. 1911 and 1915 are *karas* or wrist ornaments.

Nos. 1916, 1918 and 1920. *Pachelis* or flat bracelets.

No. 1943. A heavy bracelet with projecting knobs, worn by religious devotees.

FRAME NO. 74.

The ornaments in this frame are all in base metal, and were cast in moulds.

Nos. 1955 and 1958 and 2034 are composed of flat bars, which are united by threads ; they are worn on the upper arm (*bazuband*). Some of the bracelets have projecting grapelike bosses, as Nos. 1972, 2003, 2021, or discs with stalks like flowers, *e.g.*, Nos. 1966, 2015, 2001 and 2025.

The specimens in this frame are in popular styles, and are made in gold and silver as well as in base metal.

Case No. 75.

The metal ware which fills this case comes for the most part from Nepal. In writing of Sir E. Durand's fine collection of brass from Nepal, which filled a large room at the Imperial Institute in 1892, I made the following observations :—

" He who would understand the spirit of Hinduism, and especially the religion of the Puranas or the post-Vedic writings, must thoroughly study some such collection as this.

" There is very little of the old Aryan faith as described in the Vedas or Scriptures of the invaders of India with whom the caste system originated. It is the Nature worship of the still earlier inhabitants of India which finds expression in Nepal, especially that of Shiva or Mahadeo, the god of destruction, the third person of the Hindu Trinity, and of Parvati, his *shakti* or essence, or wife, Durga or Kali, the awful deity of Bengal.

" Hinduism, in its most terrible and superstitious forms, is rampant in Nepal, where Sati, and such like rites, are still practised."

Of the Nepal brass a critic in the *Graphic* wrote :—" Here we see barbaric art in all its wildness and luxury of detail, immensely picturesque and vigorous, but quite unrestrained in its variety and originality."

Some of the elaborate specimens shown in London, as well as the few examples in Jeypore, which the kindness of Sir E. Durand secured for the Museum, could not have been produced in Europe at any reasonable cost, as the labour of casting, by the *cire perdue* process, of such minute details is enormous. The work, I understand, can be done, but it would never pay the English workman who would be capable of doing it.

The collection contains a few hanging lamps, as for example :—

No. 2039. Below the three triple arch-shaped supports of the lamp stands a small *chhatri* or kiosk, which covers a *panch mukha* or five-headed ling, the symbol of Shiva. There are six bowls for wicks, and eight leaf pendants are suspended from the base of the lamp.

No. 2052. A lamp with a handsome arch which hangs on a long chain. The sides of the arch are flanked by *bijlis* or dragons with long tails. Ht. 10 inches.

No. 2064. A much larger specimen in which the *bijlis* are more finished and the leaf-like pendants more handsome. Ht. 13 inches.

Nos. 2055 and 2066. The leaf pendants are both perforated. Ht. 13½ inches and 13 inches respectively.

We now come to the pedestal lamps with shrines.

No. 2081. The largest, 3½ feet high, has behind it the conventional tree with flowers in bloom, while from the margin rise flamelike projections. Below is the goddess Ashtabhuja (eight-armed) Devi riding on Ganesha. The space in front is for the reception of offerings.

No. 2065. The figure at the back of this shrine is the Sun-god driving his car of seven horses, while on either side of him is a minor deity with bow bent for action. The whole of the figures appear as if in violent motion. Ht. 2 feet 5 inches.

No. 2063. The shrine back is double, and is formed by scrolls of conventional flowers. The god is the six-armed Vishnu. Ht. 3 feet 11 inches.

No. 2047. The back of this lamp is formed of large volutes or scrolls of copper. The god is Vishnu on a lotus. Ht. 2 feet 2¾ inches.

No. 2076. A lamp at the back of the case. The shrine back is formed of two trees or shrubs, Daodi (or *Chrysanthemum Indicum*) springing from two vases. Birds are perched in the foliage. The deity is the eighteen-armed Devi (Ashtadashabhuja) as Mahishasuri, or the slayer of the buffalo demon. The leaf pendants are perforated on the right. Ht. 3¼ feet.

No. 2056. Close by the last specimen is a small lamp with Shiva, and his wife Parvati, and their sons Ganesha, God of Wisdom, and Kartikeya, God of War, and immediately behind it is a perforated pedestal formed of handsome leaves, round which a cobra is entwined. Ht. 22¼ inches. There is no god in this specimen. It may be intended for the reception of a clay ling.

No. 2053 on the left has a six-sided shaft tapering upwards. Round it will also be seen the Cobra or *nag*, the snake which is so inseparably connected with the Hindu faith of Nepal, and of Shiva, and with aboriginal worship generally. The top expands into a lamp with four bowls, and is crowned with a lotus. Ht. 2 feet.

The *sikundas*, or prayer lamps, on the second and third shelves, are peculiar to Nepal. They are vases or jugs shaped to contain oil, that is taken from them, as required, by a spoon, and poured into the wick receptacle, which is overshadowed behind by an image and a shrine back. From the hind part of the vase rises a many, usually a five-headed, snake, which forms the handle, and also protects a little figure of a *naga kanya* or snake maiden. Some of the handles are formed of several snakes with interlaced tails.

In No. 2061 this is the case. The heads protect a *naga kanya*, and Ganesha overlooks the bowl, which is supported by two female figures. Ht. 10½ inches.

In No. 2059 the handle is formed of a single massive serpent. Ht. 9½ inches.

Nos. 2053, 2054, 2055, 2056, 2057, 2058 are water-pots.

No. 2058 has a spoon.

The shapes of these vessels are very classical.

No. 2040 has a fine fluted bowl with a straight spout, which springs from the mouth of a monster. Ht. 11 inches.

Nos. 2041 and 2042 are two long-necked water-bottles or *surahis* with flowers or sprigs carved in relief in diaper fashion over the bowl. Ht. 11¾ inches and 11¼ inches respectively.

No. 2043. In the centre of the second shelf is an open-work hanging basket, which is used for the reception of offerings (Ht. 11½ inches), and near it stand Nos. 2044 and 2051, two Buddhist bells, the handles of which represent a *Paripa*, with a triple head, which is used in worship. The ornament round the bell is festooned in quite an old Greek fashion, and above the rim are a number of *dorjês* or thunderbolts. Ht. 7 inches. (See Rockhill's work.)

No. 2038. Tea kettle. This is a common one of copper, such as is used in Tibet. Far more handsome ones of bronze are made, and some of them are beautifully inlaid with silver.

No. 2075 is a second prayer lamp of *yoni* * shape. Ht. 7 inches.

No. 2050. Water-pot or *kalas*. Brass and copper engraved. Ht. 5½ inches. Rs. 3-8.

It is customary, when a Chief, a noble, or a high official, in Rajputana, enters a village, for the head-man to present a rupee or two as a *nazr* or gift, while the women, with water pots (*kalas*) on their heads, sing songs of welcome. The great man usually drops the rupees into the *kalas* of the leader of the band.

No. 2069. Ditto with handle. Ht. 5¾ inches.

No. 2068. A model showing a man and his wife with three children kneeling before a lamp bowl. Ht. 4½ inches.

No. 2077. *Dhupdan* or incense-burner. Ht. 5 inches.

No. 2091. *Teldani* or lamp in the form of a handsome *tazza*. Ht. 7½ inches.

No. 2070. *Arghya*, a vessel for pouring out a libation in honour of the sun. Copper.

The remaining articles in this case are chiefly of Hindu origin.

No. 2067 is a fine *hookah* bowl with scroll ornament along each of the vertical flutes. Ht. 6 inches.

No. 2085. *Arti* or temple lamp with bowls for 15 wicks. Ht. 8¾ inches. An elephant carrying a set of 5 bowls supports a *naga kanya*, who has a similar set in her hands, and bears another on the top of the serpent's hood, which is above her head.

No. 2087. *Udbatti* or incense-burner. *Agarbatti* for holding sticks of perfumes, used in South India. Ht. 3½ inches.

No. 2094. A large *kamandalu* or fakir's water-bowl of engraved brass, with the ground filled in with red lac, made by Mohamed Hakim, of the School of Art, Jeypore. Ht. 19 inches.

No. 2096. A large brass *kamandalu* covered with chased and engraved figures (Hindu deities and women) in scrolls of the *Asparagus racemosus* deeply cut in the metal. If the interstices were filled with niello or enamel, it would be like the best Moradabad ware. Ht. 18½ inches.

No. 2097. Large shield of damascened work. False or koft. *Ganga-jamni*, in which both silver and gold leaf have been used. Ht. 16 inches.

No. 2049. Brass image. *Parvati*, wife of Shiva. Ht. 2¾ inches.

No. 2045. Brass image. Vishnu. Ht. 3 inches.

No. 2057. Brass image. Devi with shrine back. Ht. 5¼ inches.

No. 2074. *Balmakund* or the infant Krishna in brass. Worshipped by the Vallabhacharyas, or the sect which reveres Krishna as a child. Ht. 4¾ inches.

No. 2100. Water bottle or *surahi* with a peacock on the cover. Ht. 10¾ inches. Hammered brass, School of Art, Jeypore. The ribbed form of the bowl is peculiar to a number of vases of which the designs are painted on the palace walls of Amber, the old capital of Jeypore.

No. 2082. Small brass model of a *panihari* or woman carrying a *ghara* or water-pot. Brass. Ht. 5½ inches. School of Art, Jeypore.

No. 2102. Bucket. Ht. 4 inches with handle. Engraved Brass. School of Art, Jeypore.

---

* The symbol of Kali or Shakti, wife of Shiva.

No. 2084. Ornamental bracket supporting a lamp bowl. Brass.

No. 2086. Box for keeping betel leaves. Shaped leaf pipal (*Ficus religiosa*). Brass. Engraved and perforated. Ht. 1¾ inches.

No. 2093. Water-bottle or ewer with conical cover and dragon-headed spout set with garnets. Ht. 11½ inches. Brass. Engraved. School of Art, Jeypore.

No. 2090. Flat waterpot. *Jaganathi*. Engraved with a pattern of sprigs of flowers. Brass. Ht. 2¾ inches.

No. 2089. Water-vessel. *Panchpatra*. Used in worshipping to contain water for libation. Brass.

No. 2078. *Hookah* bowl with handsome vertical ribs. Bell metal. Ht. 7 inches.

No. 2079. Box. *Katordan*. Copper. Embossed and perforated with elaborate ornament. Jeypore. Ht. 11½ inches. Diam. 13½ inches.

No. 2098. Salver. Circular. Damascened with gold and silver. A fair specimen of ordinary work. Diam. 21 inches.

No. 2099. Spittoon. Brass. Engraved. Ht. 5¼ inches.

No. 2101. Long rapier with basket hilt formed by a winged monster. There is a second guard, 15 inches further down the weapon, which has numerous side-guards shaped like the heads of snakes. The blade bears the inscription "Jacobus Ollich Solingan" on one side, and on the other Jacobus Ollich. I. H. H. N. It is lent to the Museum by the Rao of Manoharpur.

No. 2103. Water-vessel with alternate, vertical, engraved and smooth ribbs. Brass. Jambu.

No. 2104. Water-bottle. *Hastawa*. Elaborately ornamented with engraved floral-designs. Old brass. Jeypore. Ht. 8 inches. Bought from Messrs. Zoroaster & Co., Jeypore.

No. 2095. Model of a cobra in the attitude of striking. The head supports a candle-stick. (A modern but not artistic addition.) Brass. Kishnagar district, Bengal. Ht. 8¼ inches.

No. 2073. Paripa with a triple head above. Surmounted by a horse's head. It is spiked to admit of its being stuck into the ground at prayer-time. Brass. Nepal.

No. 2080. Female figure with her child under her arm. Probably Jasoda and Krishna. Somewhat European in character. Brass. Ht. 8 inches. School of Art, Jeypore.

No. 2062. Toilet box or *panchpura*. Used by Mahratta women. Brass. Ht. 6 inches. A handsome specimen.

Three grotesque vessels in the forms of animals. These come from the Punjab. They are made of brass, which is painted in different colours, and are lacquered; one is a camel loaded with pack saddles, which are held up by a man to form the handle.

No. 2088. The second is a ram with the spout on the top of the head. It can be used as a *hookah*. The third is a peacock with an expanded tail. They are very quaint and curious. Below the last are some *hookahs* with bowls of leather ornamented with flat sheet brass and tin, which is cut into patterns. In two cases they are lacquered in some parts. They come from Hisar, Gujranwalla, and Kasur.

IMPERIAL INSTITUTE COLLECTION.

The Jeypore Durbar has provided a collection of the manufactures of Jeypore for exhibition at the Imperial Institute in London. Duplicates of the articles are also kept in the Jeypore Museum in order that dealers, or private individuals in England, who wish for copies, may obtain them by merely communicating the numbers to the Honorary Secretary of the Museum, or to the Principal of the School of Art in Jeypore, or to Messrs. Procter & Co., of No. 428 Oxford Street, London, and Messrs. J. Watson & Co., of Churchgate Street, Bombay, who have undertaken to execute such commissions.

The greater part of the collection was first shown at the Indian Art Metal Work Exhibition, which was held at the Imperial Institute in London in 1892.

The Jeypore Section of the brass ware is arranged on the walls of the Metal Rooms Nos. 2 and 3, in Case No. 115 in the former hall, and in Case No. 118 in the latter.

Twenty-one salvers of Mohamedan design, such as have already been described in Room No. 1, are arranged in frames above the collection of peasant jewellery in Metal Room No. 2.

There are also on the walls of this room three oval plaques with figures in high relief. They represent well-known scenes from the Mahabharata of the Emperor Akbar, *viz.*, No. 2112—Rama and his allies, the monkeys and the bears, crossing, by a bridge of stones, to Lanka or Ceylon. No. 2113, the battle of Arjuna with Susharmana, and No. 2128, Hanuman setting fire to Lanka.

Nos. 2125 and 2126 are specimens of salvers with mythological engraved subjects, and No. 2127, a circular salver with similar ornament incised in the metal and engraved.

The salvers on the walls of Room No. 3 are nearly all made after pure Hindu designs, most of which were taken from the illustrations of the Technical Art Series now in course of publication by the Government of India.

The borders are copied from the granite piers of the temple of Virabhadra at Lepaksha in the Anantapur district of the Madras Presidency, which dates from the 5th century. They belong to the Vijayanagar period of Dravidian architecture, of which the most useful feature is the running scroll, several varieties of which are represented on these trays.

Some of them are very interesting. The alternating design of No. 2168 is generally considered to be Mohamedan, but a glance, however, at the Assyrian fresco on the side wall of the eastern staircase shows that there is nothing new in the idea.

Frame No. 97.

No. 2132 is a specimen of the new kind of Moradabad brass enamel work as applied to mythological subjects. It is a circular salver with numerous figures of Hindu gods in red, green, and black round the borders and in the centre. It is effective. It was made in the Jeypore School of Art.

There are several large embossed salvers also. For example :—

2419 COFFEE POT
1033 COFFEE POT
2417 ISPAHAN VASE

2401 VASE WITH GROOVED BOWL
4313 PARSI LOTAH. SCHOOL OF ART, BOMBAY
4311 LOTAH. MADRAS SCHOOL OF ART

2058 PRAYING LAMP WITH SPOON. NEPAL
2390 CHUSKI, OR DRINKING VESSEL
TEA POT. NEPAL.

XI. BRASS WARE FROM JEYPORE, &c.

FRAME No. 105.

No. 2157, which is the largest salver in the Museum. In the centre is the personified Sun. On the border are thirty-two oval medallions in which each day of the Hindu month is represented by figures. An inner ring has sixteen medallions with one presiding deity for each day of the light or dark half of the month.

FRAME No. 104.

No. 2156 is a zodiacal salver (see No. 135, Case No. 1).

FRAME No. 113.

No. 2169 is an oval tray of embossed and perforated copper from Srinagar, Kashmir.

CHAPTER IV.

METAL ROOM No. III.

Case No. 115 contains a number of small brass vessels, models of animals, etc., some of which are already exhibited in the general collection. Of the rest, the following are the most interesting:—

On the top shelf are a number of small brass models of Indian animals, such as elephants, camels, boars, fighting rams, horses, the rhinoceros, monkeys, and a few birds.

In the centre line are specimens of *koft* or false damascening (Nos. 2000 to 2004).

Nos. 2202 and 2205 are vessels of copper with silver crustæ, which were copied at the Jeypore School of Art from Tanjore originals.

On the second shelf the principal specimens are (No. 2235) a bottle of engraved brass shaped like a cock (No. 2234), a copy of a Russian censor (No. 2254), and a lobed vase with birds, which serve as handles.

We have next a group of five rose-water sprinklers of different shapes and designs, all of which are good.

In the centre are two small *koft* trays (Nos. 2236 and 2237).

No. 2245 is a specimen of *tah-i-nishan* or true damascening.

No. 2238 is a copy in brass of a silver *ghara* or water-vessel, which was exhibited at Lahore in 1882. It is covered with diaper ornament on a frosted ground, and is of Turkish design.

A handsome water-bottle of a similar character stands a little further on in the case (No. 2243).

No. 2241 is an *atrdan* in brass—a reproduction of No. 854 in the silver case (No. 44).

On the floor of the case are three salvers—No. 2255, with Krishna and Radha in the centre; No. 2257, copied from No. 1024 in Case No. 57; No. 2262, with Garuda killing a monster. All the above are in brass repoussé.

No. 2258, engraved brass, is a copy of salver No. 1005 in Case No. 57, and No. 2265 is a fine *atrdan* in brass.

Nos. 2256*a* and 2256*b* are moulds, which show the method of making a pair of zinc bracelets at one casting by the *cire perdue* process.*

CASE No. 116.

Case No. 116 is devoted chiefly to a few purchases, which were made at the Lahore Exhibition of 1894.

On the top shelf are a few domestic vessels of brass with incised ornament, which further illustrate the desire for decoration which is innate amongst so many of the Hindus of low caste (see Case No. 68, Nos. 2268 to 2273).

At the east end of the shelf is a specimen of old Moradabad ware. It is a *hookah* (No. 2267). The diaper ornament is very similar to that of the Sanganir chintzes.

In the centre of the second shelf are four fine examples of old Moradadad *hookah* bowls (Nos. 2279 to 2282).

* For a full description of the process, see Proceedings of the Iron and Steel Institute for 1886.

No. 2280 has very fine floral diapers in silver and gold.

The zig-zag ornament on No. 2281 is of a very ancient form which is common in Egyptian art.

On No. 2282 is the Kashmir shawl pattern. Close to the above are two old examples of the lacquered and enamelled ware of Srinagar (Nos. 2283 and 2284).

Close by are a number of brass figures of animals, reptiles, and insects (Nos. 2285 to 2302) from Sivagunga in the Madura district, Madras Presidency.

No. 2277 is a coffee-pot or ewer of white metal of good classical design from Peshawar.

On the lower shelf are a few specimens of engraved and embossed copper ware from Kashmir (Nos. 2310 to 2312).

Two very curious iron tongs used by religious devotees for sacrificial purposes are on the same shelf (Nos. 2314 and 2315).

Near them are two copies of Tibetan tea-pots of excellent design, with handles and spouts in the form of dragons or sea monsters. They were made in Jeypore.

A small tray (No. 2317) and *chilam* (No. 2313), set with turquoises and garnets, came from Bokhara, where these stones are largely used for such purposes. H. R. H. the Duke of Coburg (Edinburgh) sent a fine set of harness enriched in this manner to the Imperial Institute Exhibition in 1892. It was presented to him by the Emperor of Russia, who received it from Bokhara.

The great Case No. 118, close to the west door of the room, but in the adjacent corridor, contains the larger specimens of the Institute Series, of which the principal are as follow :—

On the top shelf stand three large ewers (Nos. 2385 to 2387).

On the second shelf, in the centre, is a fine copy of a Ganges-water vessel or *chambu* (No. 2392), of which numerous specimens will be described when we come to Case No. 323in the Mythological Room.

No. 2389 is a handsome box with fine oval medallions of flowers in repoussé. Near them are several Rajput drinking vessels (*chuski*) and a Hindu water-pot with bold mythological figures in niches.

The third shelf is filled with handsome objects, most of which are copies of specimens in Case No. 57.

Nos. 2406 and 2410 are female figures (*sakhi*) holding lamps, which were copied from old temple lamps from Udaipur.

No. 2408 is perhaps the finest vessel in the case. It is a *gamla* or water-pot with three rows of figures in repoussé round the bowl. The one in the centre represents the ten incarnations of Krishna in niches; above are the great gods in their celestial cars, and below them are the personified planets. On the cover small figures represent the *gopies* or milkmaids circling round Krishna and Radha or, according to some, the Ras Mandala or heavenly sphere.

On the fourth shelf are numerous fine water-bottles and vases.

No. 2429 is a kettle supported by monkeys—an example of what some have styled debased art, but which finds frequent purchasers amongst strangers.

Nos. 2436 and 2418 are reproductions in brass of Tibetan tea-pots.

No. 2420 is a water-bottle with very delicately worked bands of flowers round the bowl.

At the bottom of the case are eight salvers (Nos. 2439 to 2446), showing, in all the different stages, the process of making a repoussé salver.

No. 2448 is a particularly fine ewer with diaper ornament ; and the next two vessels are good examples of Nepalese ewers.

Nos. 2453 to 2458 are Turkish coffee-pots and cream jugs.

EAST CORRIDOR.

WALL FRAME NO. 117.

Most of the articles in this frame are ornaments for the arm.

Nos. 2319 and 2346 are hollowed to contain some small balls, which rattle as the wearer moves her arm.

Nos. 2328 and 2330 are ornaments which are fastened on to the upper arm by means of cords of silk or cotton. They are good in design. There are a number of rings at the bottom of the frame, some of which, as for example Nos. 2352, 2353 and 2373, have inscriptions upon them, and are used as signet rings. It is the custom in India for soldiers, officials, and servants of all classes to make impressions of their seals on the pay rolls when they are unable to sign their names.

Nos. 2358, 2359 and 2372 should contain pieces of glass. Females wear such rings, and, at a glance in them, can re-arrange their hair or ornaments when they are out of place.

WALL FRAME NO. 119.

This frame is devoted to rings, bracelets, waist-belts, and miscellaneous ornaments.

The waist-belt or *kangati* (Nos. 2461, 2467 and 2480) is worn by both men and women, and is generally composed, as in the specimens, of several chains or cords which are united by clasps or bands. The ends are united by a screw, which in the East, as elsewhere observed, turns from left to right, or in the opposite direction to that adopted in the West. For the connection of the chains with the universality of certain forms of ornament, the reader should turn to the notes on page 20 (Frame No. 41, Room No. 1) regarding the Tara brooch, as the cords of these waist-belts are similar to those attached to the Irish jewel. Phœnician chains of the same kind have been found.

No. 2468 is a common ornament which is worn on the head. There are two bell-shaped earrings, with pendants, which are worn in the ear, and part of the weight is borne by chains which are attached to the hair and cross the head.

No. 2473 is a perforated ornament of some skill in design, which is worn by Nagar women of the Bombay Presidency on their heads, generally on the top-knot.

WALL FRAME NO. 120.

No. 2526 is a very fine salver on which are represented two *apsaras* or heavenly nymphs pouring out wine in honour of heroes. It is taken from the cenotaph of Maharaja Sawai Jai Singh, the founder of Jeypore, at Gettore near the capital. A special certificate was awarded for this design by the Society for the Encouragement and Preservation of Indian Art at the Imperial Institute Exhibition of 1892.

WALL FRAME NO. 121.

A circular tray, with perforated border and raised foliage and geometrical design in the centre, comes from the Madras School of Art. The style is in vogue at Kumbakonam in the Southern Presidency.

WALL FRAMES NOS. 122, 123, 124.

These frames are filled with perhaps the most regal designs for ornaments in the whole collection. They are all ankle and foot ornaments.

Nos. 2530 and 2532 are anklets or *karas* of twisted strands ; the former terminates in the heads of sea monsters (*azdaha*) ; the latter in knobs. Both forms are very classical, and may be seen on the early stone images in the Museum. Similar anklets were worn in Phœnicia and perhaps other countries. The anklets, made up of perforated pieces which are strung on cords known as *paezeb*, are very fine. The best specimens are perhaps Nos. 2534 and 2544 in Frame No. 122, and No. 2573 in Frame No. 123. The above are worn in the North-Western Provinces and Oudh. There are numerous specimens of a circular ornament (*anwat*) which is worn by means of a toe ring on the front of the foot. The best are Nos. 2539 and 2531 in Frame No. 122.

In Frame No. 124 are a number of curious toe rings, also termed *anwat*, which are worn on the front of the great toe, and are kept in place by a projecting spike which passes under the second toe. They are worn by women of the lower classes in Northern India. Some of the flat anklets, which are cast in one piece to imitate the *paezeb* (Nos. 2562, 2564, etc., Frame No. 123), must, from their shape, be very awkward to wear.

Many of the foot ornaments are very massive. The W-shaped anklets (Nos. 2608, 2610 and 2612) are generally worn by Bhil and Gujar women. A full set may weigh several pounds.

Frames Nos. 125, 126, 133 and 134 are handsome panels of copper with foliage and birds in *alto relievo.* Such work is made for mountings on chairs and doors at Kumbakonam in Madras. The present specimens are the work of pupils of the School of Art in that presidency.

FRAME NO. 127.

This contains small single and double-headed combs of sandalwood, blackwood, etc. The former are chiefly made by Punjabis at Jeypore and Ajmere ; the latter, some of which are inlaid with wire or silver or lead, come from Nagina in the North-Western Provinces.

No. 2647 has a small sliding panel, which in this case conceals a mirror, but in some specimens perfumed oil takes its place.

FRAME NO. 128.

Besides a few combs, there are several rosaries of sandalwood.

Nos. 2666 and 2669 are necklaces of small shells, and anklets, which are cut from larger ones, from Dacca.

Frame No. 129.

At the top of the case are three rows of stamps, and blocks of bell metal, which are used by jewellers for making ornaments in all metals.

Below them are two blowpipes and several massive anklets.

No. 3361 is a fine carved blackwood chair from Ahmedabad.

Frame No. 130.

This frame is filled with rude lac beads, and even paper ornaments, which are worn by the very lowest classes and aboriginal tribes, as well as by children in the towns after fairs, etc.

Frame No. 131.

This frame contains ankle and foot ornaments. The most interesting are little oblong shields which are worn by means of rings on the toes. They are termed *bichhua* (Nos. 2807 to 2813, 2823 to 2831, etc., etc).

No. 2769. Five of these rings are attached to a plate which rests on the front of the foot.

Frame No. 132.

This frame contains a miscellaneous collection of large rude bead ornaments which are put on the necks of horses.

Nos. 2853 to 2868 are rings set with rough gems.

Nos. 2909 to 2931. Hair-pins from Kashmir.

Nos. 2932 to 2941. Anklets, etc.

Frames Nos. 135, 136, 137.

These frames contain ankle and foot ornaments. The most interesting are the anklets known as *santh* (No. 2963 in Frame No. 135, and Nos. 3040, 3050, 3080 and 3084), all of which are cast in one piece by the *cire perdue* process, as described at page 42 (Case No. 115).

Frame No. 138.

The two salvers in this frame were made at the Madras School of Art. They are of brass, inlaid with copper, arranged in medallions and scrolls. The ornament is chiefly floral, but birds are introduced.

Frames Nos. 139, 140, 146, 147.

These frames contain small circular trays from Jeypore similar to Nos. 956, 958, 968, 974, 979 and 985 in Case No. 56 in Room No. 1.

Frame No. 141.

The large brass salver in this frame is a good example of Damascus work. There are numerous panels of figures and Arabic characters in repoussé over the whole ground.

Frame No. 142.

We have in this case another salver with inscriptions in silver foil in relief. The silver is made to adhere in the manner of the dovetailing of the crustæ in Tanjore work (see page 11, Metal Room No. I, Case No. 14).

FRAME NO. 143.

The circular salver in this frame is a much finer example of the work described in Frame No. 121

FRAME NO. 144.

We have here a salver from Constantinople with fine arabesque ornament and inscription in relief.

FRAME NO. 145.

An octagonal tray of similar workmanship to No. 3094 in Frame No. 143.

FRAME NO. 148.

Returning to the east corridor, we come to a large copper vase which was made at the School of Art in Bombay. It is a handsome vessel, and is covered with fine classical ornament in relief, which is taken from the caves at Ajunta.

CASE NO. 149.

Case No. 149 contains a series of small models in papier-mâche of the heads of men of the principal castes and occupations in Rajputana, and especially in Jeypore. They are careful studies from life, and on each is placed the turban or *pagri* of cotton which is usually worn by the person represented. Many of the faces are scarred with small-pox marks. In some instances a blind eye is shown. These defects are not exaggerated, as before the spread of vaccination the disease raged unchecked, and often severely mutilated many who escaped death.

The turbans are arranged in a great variety of ways, and are of many colours, while some of them are most picturesque.

Nos. 3105 to 3136 represent Brahmans.

Nos. 3137 to 3138, 3152, 3167 represent Rajputs.

Nos. 3139 to 3150, 3153 to 3166 represent Banias, and the remainder, Nos. 3169 to 3173, represent the minor castes, Musalmans, etc.

Collections of this kind have been supplied to several museums. They were first made at Jeypore for the author of this handbook. *Pagris* are made on wooden blocks, and, when not in use, are also kept upon them by wealthy persons ; but every man can make up his own turban with more or less taste. On special occasions, as marriages, etc., the *pagriband*, who is generally a tailor, is applied to, so as to secure a better effect.

Turbans may be worn in different ways, as, for example, if placed obliquely (*banki*) on the head, the wearer is considered a fast man. In Jeypore about 18 or 20 yards of cloth, 9 inches wide, are used in coloured *pagris*. For a coloured turban a white *pagri* is taken, and dyed by an elaborate process. For each colour pieces of the stuff are tied by women with thread into knots and dyed separately. Some of the patterns are very elaborate and pretty. The colours are nearly always fugitive. At marriages, and on festive occasions, red, yellow, and bright colours are used. For mourning, black, dark red, ash colour, and sombre tints are used if the father is alive. White can be worn at visits of condolence if a man's own father is dead. Old men generally wear a white *pagri.*

Nos. 3193 to 3195 are small models of turbans worn by the Maharana, who is the ruling Chief of Meywar or Udaipur. These turbans give an air of great dignity to the wearer.

Nos. 3226 to 3228 are Mahratta turbans from Indore. Many yards of cloth are wound in flat bands to form a huge kind of dish round the head.

Nos. 3218 to 3225 are caps worn by Mohamedans. Further details are not needed, as the labels give all the information that is necessary.

At the bottom of the case are arranged a number of specimens of shell work as applied to baskets, trays, etc., from the Seychelle Islands. There are also grass mats, bonnets, etc., from the same place.

As regards papier-mâche figures, they are also made in Jeypore of large size, and are chiefly used at a kind of miracle play which is acted in the principal bazár. It represents the appearance of the man-lion (Narasinha) or fourth incarnation of Vishnu.

The appearance of the boar incarnation (Vāraha Avatarā) is also sometimes acted in the same way.

CASE NO. 150.

This case contains a somewhat miscellaneous collection, chiefly consisting of ivory, tortoise shell, and horn-work from Vizagapatam in the Madras Presidency, and of similar work, with the addition of wire, from Bombay and Surat on the west side of India. In the former, according to Dr. Bidie, "the surface of the ivory is generally adorned with etchings in black of mythological figures very well executed, or with floral forms in light and shade, which are copies of European designs."

Sir G. Birdwood states that the Bombay work was introduced from Persia.

At one end of the case are specimens of Tarkashi wire-work from Mainpuri in the North-West Provinces.

Foliage, figure, and geometrical designs are formed of fine brass wire, which is let into minute channels in hard shisham (*Dalbergia latifolia*) wood. It is a form of damascening well known in other parts of the world. I met with specimens in Constantinople which had been made in Broussa in Anatolia, a district of Asia Minor. Bronze was damascened in this way in Egypt at a very early period. There is also a good deal of Hoshiarpur work, which is ivory inlay, with occasional use of brass, on shisham wood. The designs are floral for the most part.

The case also contains a few examples of tortoise-shell card cases, combs, etc. (Nos. 3273 to 3277), from Kandy in Ceylon. A box formed of a painted cocoanut comes from Sawantwadi (No. 3278). Two beautiful bezique markers from Japan are choice examples of modern work. The mother-o'-pearl inlay is very minute, but exquisite in colour and design.

3404 CARVED BLACKWOOD PAPER KNIFE. BIJNORE.
3260 PICTURE FRAME, IVORY INLAY. HOSHIARPUR.
3373 PAINTED WOODEN FIGURE. SURAT.
3293 SMALL IVORY COUNTER, WITH ETCHED FIGURE.
3343 TORTOISESHELL AND IVORY FRETWORK. VIZIGAPATAM.
3323 BOMBAY INLAY.
3338 BOX, ACACIA WOOD INLAID WITH BRASS WIRE. MAINPURI.

XV. IVORY INLAY, &c.

Nos. 3344 and 3345 are fan handles of ivory. The fans are made of *khas-khas* grass (*Andropogon muriaticus*). They came from Mairtain Marwar, a place long celebrated for its ivory carving, chiefly of bracelets.

Nos. 3351 to 3354 are fans of which the blades are made of talc. These slips are cleverly etched with figures of dancing girls, etc. They are made at Trichinopoly in the Madras Presidency.

The following examples of the different kinds of work just described are specially worthy of attention :—

Nos. 3243. A watch stand. Ht. 20½". A distorted horn is carved into the head of a stag and fitted with tynes. The mouth holds a brass serpent, a cobra. The pedestal, also of horn, has embedded in it fragments of the same material which are curiously carved. It was made at Vizagapatam by Chinna Virana.

No. 3244. Model of a palanquin. Sandalwood inlaid with ivory and metal in the well-known style known as Bombay inlay. L. 29", Ht. 8½". Made at Billimora, near Surat, by Sorabji.

No. 3245. Model of a water-bottle of cocoanut, painted with outlines of birds in scrolls of leaves in silver. Ht. 10½".

Nos. 3262 and 3263. Hoshiarpur rulers of shisham wood inlaid with ivory. Each 20" long.

Nos. 3264 and 3265. A pair of bathing clogs.

No. 3337. Inlaid walking staff. L. 4ft. Maker, Kuniya Lall.

No. 3268. Walking stick formed of disks of betelnut (*Areca catechu*), with top of carved ivory in the shape of a tiger's head. Maker, Sultan, Khairati, of Bugru, near Jeypore.

No. 3270 and 3271. A pair of carved shisham wood bathing clogs, inlaid sparingly, but tastefully, with ivory. Brought from Kashmir.

Nos. 3339 and 3340. A pair of bathing clogs. Mainpuri. When pressed, the ivory top of the toe-pin expands to form a lotus.

No. 3335. A salver. Diameter 11½." In the centre is an eagle with expanded wings. Maker, Gunga Pershad, Lohar (*Madar Darwaza*). Mainpuri.

No. 3278. A box in the form of a vase or water-bottle cocoanut painted in different colours with Hindu deities in medallions, which are formed by flowers. Sawantwadi.

No. 3286. A book cover. Sandalwood, carved. Subject : Animals and birds, in floral scroll work. Border of Bombay inlay. Maker, Jai Raj, Khatri. Bought from Jamsetji Shapurji, Bombay.

No. 3287. An album cover. Sandalwood, with panels of deeply carved ebony Subject : Temples and houses in the midst of foliage, flowers, and fruit. Excellent work The carvings are conventional and in high relief. Border of Bombay inlay. Made in Surat.

No. 3289. A book slide. Sandalwood, enriched with ivory fret carving in which the principal figures are further ornamented with etching in black lines. Vizagapatam.

No. 3279. A handsome stationery case of dark shisham wood with fittings of sandalwood. The outside is beautifully inlaid with floral panels of ivory. Made in Mysore.

Presented by H. H. the Maharaja of Mysore in commemoration of his visit to the Jeypore Museum.

No. 3282. A card box. Sandalwood, with Bombay inlay. Four inner receptacles contain sandalwood and ivory counters, which are also enriched with Bombay inlay.

No. 3295. A collection of patterns of Bombay inlay on sandalwood. Forty-six specimens. These illustrate all the best designs. They were made by workmen in the employ of Messrs. J. P. Watson & Co., Bombay.

No. 3330. A walking stick of betel-nut (*Areca catechu*) disks.

No. 3348. A walking stick. Shaft of spirally carved blackwood. There is a little ivory inlay near the handle and lower end.

No. 3346. An inkstand and stationery cabinet. Ebony with rather rude ornament of small pieces of ivory inlay. Made in Bengal.

No. 3344. Handles for khas-khas grass (*Andropogon muriaticus*) fans. Shisham wood and ivory cylinders, the latter coloured in red bands and etched rings. There are two small mirrors at the ends. Made at Mairta in Marwar.

Nos. 3351 to 3353. Fans of talc in gilt frames of cane with coloured spun silk edges. The talc is cleverly etched with figures of dancing girls. Trichinopoly, Madras.

CHAPTER V.

CENTRE ROOM, GROUND FLOOR.

THIS hall contains examples of wood-carving, and of nearly all the minor industrial arts of India.

In the large central case at the east end specimens of metal ware from oriental countries, and reproductions of fine examples of European art, are shown with two objects in view—first, in order that their influence upon, and connection with, Indian work may be studied ; and, secondly, to enable the local artist not only to see what other nations look upon as artistic, but to give him an opportunity of observing the superiority in many respects, especially in finish, of the productions of those countries over his own. He will learn that mechanical dexterity, and facility of enriching surfaces, are not alone sufficient, but that there must be originality and knowledge, both of which require better education than he possesses, if his artistic creations are to live. The great west case in the same room does for the pottery and porcelain in the adjacent room what this eastern one does for metal in the first hall. The chintzes in the tops of the side cases were all made at Sanganir, a town about eight miles to the south of Jeypore. Reference has already been made to the mischief which has been done to this industry by the introduction of machinery, and still more by the use of crude aniline dyes.

In former days the place was flourishing, because the prince and his nobles, as well as the common people, all wore chintzes, which were at first stamped on the coarse cloth or *rezi* of the country. The first sign of change was the introduction of English cotton cloth, which was softer and cheaper, but certainly not so æsthetic in appearance, although perhaps the *couleur d'ivoire* of the ground of some kinds of the former stuffs looked better than on the coarse local cloth ; then came the Manchester commercial traveller, who copied the designs, and undersold the Sanganir dyer and the Jeypore bania for whom he worked ; and at last were introduced the aniline dyes, which could be applied over and over again to the same pieces of fabric, according as fashion, or the fancy of the wearer, changed.

The cloth is provided by the *bania* or dealer in Jeypore, who selects a pattern, which is stamped by the dyers and their families in their homes at Sanganir.

CASE NO. 151.

This case contains wood-carving and painted figures, chiefly from Western and Southern India.

No. 3362. A vase on a pedestal with two handles. Blackwood, carved all over with leaves and fruit. In the bowl the carving is cut quite through the wood. Ht. 16". Ahmedabad.

No. 3363. A carved sandalwood fan. The upper part is formed like a peacock with a folding tail. Indore.

Three carved cocoanut goblets, with covers, ornamented with three medallions cut into groups of figures, as, for example, No. 3364, Krishna playing the flute. Ceylon.

No. 3366. Three ditto, with figures of elephants and other animals carved round the bowl.

No. 3401. A very much larger and finer specimen with perforated cover. A band of animals runs round the top of the bowl, and below it are the ten incarnations of Vishnu.

PAINTED, GILT, AND LACQUERED WOODEN TOYS FROM SURAT.

No. 3365. A country cart with domed top, drawn by a pair of bullocks.

No. 3370. A peasant woman with two water-pots on her head.

No. 3373. Ditto.

No. 3371. A grotesque bird with expanded tail.

No. 3593. An elephant with a *mahout* or driver.

No. 3394. Ditto with state *hawdah* or seat.

No. 3395. A *pakhal* bullock with *bhisti*. This is a bullock carrying two large water-skins and the waterman.

No. 3406. A peacock.

No. 3407. A female figure balanced on the top of a pole by two elephants placed at either end of a carved iron bar.

No. 3408. A camel with kettle-drums and drummer.

Nos. 3372 to 3383. Specimens of lac ware from Birbhum, Bengal.

No. 3372. A watch stand.

No. 3384. A paper weight.

Nos. 3374 to 3383. Ten napkin rings.

No. 3385. A glove box, carved in a very bold fashion with scrolls and leaves. L. 16", W. 5", Ht. 3¾". Bikanir.

Nos. 3368 and 3386. A pair of carved candlesticks of ebony. The patterns are very minute. Bijnor, N.-W. P.

No. 3400. A handsome octagonal cabinet or tea caddy, with delicate conventional patterns of flowers cut in black ebony. Nagina, near Bijnor, N.-W. P.

No. 3399. A travelling clock case. Nagina.

No. 3398. A picture frame for three small portraits, with pierced carved borders; blackwood. Ahmedabad.

No. 3396. Ditto for one portrait.

No. 3397. Ditto ditto.

No. 3367. An oblong casket with three-sided top. Ht. 8", L. 11½", W. 7". Blackwood, with deeply cut figures of dragons, demons and birds, enriched with engraved white metal hinges, etc. Kandy, Ceylon.

No. 3388. A fly whisk, with carved sandalwood handle. Rampore, near Indore.

No. 3389. A carved octagonal sandalwood glove box. On the top is a building in the midst of foliage. L. 11".

No. 3391. A carved note-paper box. L. 8¼", W. 6", Ht. 3¾". On the lid are two landscapes in wreaths of flowers.

No. 3390. A sherbet spoon. Leaf-shaped blade with perforated carved handles. Very delicate. Made at Umballa. Delicate spoons of this kind are made in Persia.

No. 3392. A carved sandalwood whisk with plume composed of fine threads of the same. Bharatpur. Made only for the Chief.

No. 3369. A goblet with very curiously carved bowl. Dark blackwood. Kandy, Ceylon.

No. 3405. A photograph of the fort at Trichinopoly in a frame of local dried seeds and fruits. Varnished imitation of work at one time much in vogue in England at seaside places.

Nos. 341 to 3413. Four turned and lacquered wood bedstead legs made in Khandela in Shekhawati, the northern province of Jeypore. Very much of this kind of work is made in Rajputana.

No. 3414. Octagonal tray on feet. Wood painted and lacquered; ornament floral. Trichinopoly, Madras.

No. 3415. Book cover. Carved sandalwood. A fine specimen of Surat work.

No. 3416. Burmese bowl, filled with lacquered balls and dice from Central India.

No. 3402. Jewel box, with drawers and numerous small inner boxes, all carved. All round it run deeply cut figures in niches, and on the lid is represented Arjuna in his car slaying his enemies. A very fine specimen. Ht. 12", L. 18," W. 12". Made by Krishna Appa Shivaji. District Mysore.

Nos. 3403 and 3404. A pair of carved ebony wood paper knives. Bijnor, North-Western Provinces. L. 16".

No. 3419. Plaque. Ivory and mother-o'-pearl, carved inlay, on black lacquer. Modern ordinary work. Japan. L. 28", W. 19".

No. 3418. Work box. Varnished nutmeg wood. Ceylon.

Nos. 3420 to 3423. Four *charpai* legs from Khandala (see No. 33).

Nos. 3424 to 3431. Another set.

Nos. 3432 and 3433. Two bedstead legs, carved like pillars.

No. 3434. Carved wood box. L. 12" × 8" × 4". Saharanpur, North-Western Provinces. Made of *Wrightia tomentosa* wood.

No. 3435. Carved camphor wood panel. L. 2' 11", W. 2¼'. From Japan. Subject: A female sitting on a dragon approaching a sage.

No. 3417. Lacquered fan shaped like a half palm leaf (papier mâche), and decorated with sprays of gilt flowers, from Hyderabad in the Deccan.

CASE NO. 152.

The first recess case in the centre room contains brackets, paper knives, spoons, forks, and other articles from Saharanpur in the North-Western Provinces. They are carved into various patterns in the wood of the *Wrightia tomentosa*.

FRAMES NOS. 154 AND 155.

In these are shown two fine specimens of elaborate and minute carving in walnut wood from Simla.

RECESS CASE NO. 156.

At the top of the case, below two pieces of Sanganir chintz, are several octagonal wooden trays (*kishti*), which were painted and lacquered at Tilhar, near Shahjehanpur

(Nos. 3455 to 3459). Such trays are used for the presentation of gifts at durbars or wedding feasts.

Next to them are sets of the well-known square baskets from Ceylon, which are made to fit into each other, forming nests of from three to ten specimens. Most of them are ornamented by using different colours of gold thread in the material (Nos. 3460 to 3464).

A cane tray and basket box, of which the top is fastened by means of a peculiar screw arrangement, came from Bandar Abbas in the Persian Gulf (Nos. 3465 to 3467).

Grass trays from Peshawar (Nos. 3469 to 3478), cane baskets from Thana in the Bombay Presidency (Nos. 3470 to 3477), and grass mats and boxes from Japan (Nos. 3476 to 3479, etc.), illustrate useful economic manufactures.

PILLAR FRAMES NO. 157.

As in the Museum space is so limited, each of the pillars on which the galleries rest is also utilized for the support of twelve small frames for textiles, photographs, etc.

Nos. 3485 to 3562 are the illustrations of Sir G. Birdwood's South Kensington Manual on the Industrial Arts of India.

No. 3563. Here also are 96 circular Indian playing cards (*ganjifa*). Small cards can be easily procured, but the man who made these larger ones (3½ inches in diameter) is now dead, and has left no one to do the work. They are painted in body colour and lacquered.

Nos. 3564 to 3568. Five coloured drawings of floral decoration from the palace at Amber. Amongst them is one of the conventional representation of the lotus in water—an old Turanian design.

Nos. 3569 to 3582. A series of photographs of Burmese art ware, and

No. 3583. A copy of the first page of a famous copy of the Koran, which is now at Ulwar.

GARNETS CASE NO. 158.

Case No. 158 contains a large collection of garnet jewellery from a State factory in Jeypore, which a few years ago was under the management of Mr. S. J. Tellery. This institution was abolished, and the trade and manufacture are now in the hands of dealers and bankers in the town. There is also a large trade in the rough garnets, which are in great demand in Europe and India. The best stones are now quarried in the south-west corner of the Jeypore State, not far from Rajmehal on the Banas river. The matrix, in which the crystals are imbedded, is mica schist or serpentine. The selected stones are generally polished into carbuncles or cabochons, which are known as tallow tops in the trade, because they are convex above and concave or flat below, and resemble drops of tallow. Many stones are also cut into facets for rings, necklaces, bracelets, etc., and a special class of work-people in Jeypore is employed in stringing them on silk for neck and wrist ornaments.

The garnet, according to a great authority, possesses all the virtues of the noblest gems, except rarity, and consequent intrinsic value.

Gold of course forms the best setting for the stone, but silver is used for the cheaper ornaments, both in this country and in Europe.

The following exhibits may be more particularly studied in connection with the foregoing remarks :—

No. 3584. A cameo portrait of H. H. Sir Sawai Madho Singh, Bahadur, G.C.S.I., the ruling Chief of Jeypore. It is mounted in silver.

Nos. 3588 and 3594. Two small models in silver of Hindu water-vessels, which are set with garnets.

No. 3585, a pepper castor ; No. 3592, a salt cellar ; and No. 3596, a ring for a table napkin,—to show the use of the stone in decorating domestic plate.

On the front of the stand in the case are a number of cheap silver brooches, many of inartistic European design, which found a ready sale in India and Europe. Some of the necklaces below these are more oriental in character, as for example No. 3624, which is taken from the Burmese design for a forehead ornament described in Case No. 15 (Nos. 284 and 327), Metal Room I. Below them again are collar and shirt studs, clasps, pins, and sleeve links.

On the upper portion of the stand at the back of the case are numerous specimens of carbuncles and garnets in the rough from different quarries in Rajputana.

On the back of the stand are arranged armlets (No. 3752) of crystal from Tonk, and carbuncles from Jeypore, with more necklaces of carbuncles as well as of plasma (Nos. 3756 and 3755), which resembles jade, but is much softer, especially when first taken from the quarries, the principal of which are at Shahpur in the Punjab.

No. 3753. Necklaces of carnelian (No. 3754), of bloodstone, heliotrope and lapis lazuli (Nos. 5723, 3729 and 3730), and of amber from Pomerania.

PILLAR FRAMES NO. 159.

The principal exhibits are (Nos. 3764 to 3766) some bazar paintings from Nepal, a set of miniature paintings on ivory plaques from Trichinopoly (Nos. 3767 to 3816), and one from Delhi (No. 3817), subject : The Kutb Minar. The former are much inferior to the latter. The Delhi artists produce excellent work in an old-fashioned stiff manner. The subjects treated are the well-known buildings in the great Moghul capitals, and portraits of a conventional type of the emperors and their female relations and courtiers. The Trichinopoly artist represents the great rock-fort at his capital, and also temples, and birds and beasts.

Nos. 3818 to 4287. Following these come a series of designs for blocks for the chintz cloths of Sanganir. They are old and afford many hints for the artistic treatment of fabrics. This is a branch of design in which Indians excel.

CASE NO. 160.

The centre show case at the east end of the middle room contains a number of interesting objects, which have been brought together, principally, to illustrate the origin of many Indian arts in metal or their connection with similar work in other countries.

Reproductions of masterpieces of European artists of different periods are also shown, in order that the local workmen may examine what has been thought excellent in other countries than their own and at different periods of time. They will see that true art can always be recognized, and also note where their own work fails.

The jewel box (No. 4291) is a good example of Constantinople (Stamboul) embossed metal work, which is richly encrusted with coral and turquoises.

Nos. 4317, 4318 and 4319. These form a set of gilt brass vessels, coffee-pots, etc., such as are used in Constantinople by the Turks.

No. 4313 is an engraved and chased brass water-pot or *lotah* for the use of Parsis. It, as well as No. 4367, a copper plaque; No. 4368, a carved wood table; and No. 4369, a carved box, were made in the technical workshops of the School of Art at Bombay, and are examples of the improvement, as to finish and design, which such an institution, when rightly managed, may effect.

Nos. 4315 and 4312. Burmese bowls, mounted on three *kailins* or dragons, a European innovation, which was supposed to be suitable to the characteristic ornament of the silver ware, and to the weird ideas of the Burmese.

Nos. 4310 and 4307. Rose-water sprinklers. These came from Jodhpore. They are fair examples of the massive parcel-gilt silver plate which was formerly made in Rajputana. The designs are bold.

No. 4309 is a little water-vessel from the same place, which is enriched with outlines in niello.

No. 4308, a small silver mace, illustrates the favourite mode of ornamenting staves, etc., with embossed patterns. It is called a *danka,* and is used by boys when dancing on the day called Ganesh Chouth.

We now come to some reproductions of old Roman plate by Messrs. Elkington & Co. The originals were found in 1868 by Prussian soldiers near Hildesheim. They are now in the museum in Berlin.

No. 4306 is a cup or "cylix."

No. 4305 is a patera with a seated figure of Minerva in high relief at the bottom of the bowl. This is a very handsome piece.

No. 4304 is also a cup termed "Cantharos." The handles are formed of lions' heads, and the body is ornamented with six masks and Bacchic symbols.

No. 4395, a small salt cellar, and No. 4396, an oblong tray, are less interesting.

No. 4300 is known as the "Cellini Cup." The original is supposed to be the work of the great Italian master, Benvenuto Cellini. It should be compared with (No. 4298) the copy of the Jamnitzar cup, which was the work of a celebrated goldsmith of Nuremburg (Nos. 1508 to 1585), and with a candlestick (an original) in silver gilt enamel (No. 4303 *bis*), which dates from the beginning of the 18th century.

No. 4297 is a copy of another famous piece, a cup embossed with the subject of the apotheosis of Homer. The original was found at Herculaneum, and was made before the Christian era.

We now return to oriental work, and first to No. 4295, a painted metal water-vessel from Persia (No. 4292), a spittoon of painted and lacquered metal from the same place, and then to a vase (No. 4294), and other objects (Nos. 4325 and 4326) of iron damascened in gold, with the principal designs deeply chiselled out of the metal. No. 4327 is a reproduction of the sherbet bowl (No. 4325), which was made in Jeypore by a man who had not done that kind of work before. It is difficult to distinguish the copy from the original.

Nos. 4293, 4322 and 4323 are examples of iron bowls, etc., enriched with plain designs in gold wire (true damascening), all from Teheran in Persia.

The bowl (No. 4321) and the box of engraved copper (No. 4332) are from Yemen in Arabia. An engraved brass bowl from Arabia (No. 4333), a bowl cover (No. 4335), and a small cylindrical vessel (No. 4337), the two latter from Mosul, are worth study in connection with the art of damascening.

No. 4334. A silver Byzantine church bowl, with figures in relief, serves to connect Persian with Byzantine art.

No. 4364, neck chains; No. 4365, a dagger; and No. 4366, a thumb ring, are examples of old Jodhpore silver work.

Nos 4370, 4380. Large shisham wood coffers, covered with bold carving, may be compared with Nos. 4368 and 4369 from the School of Art with some interest. They were made in Shekhawati (North Jeypore) by carpenters, whose chief business is to ornament the doors and window frames of the merchants, who live in the large towns. The work is bold and effective; but the badly chosen wood illustrates another defect of Hindu workmen, *viz.*, utter carelessness in selection of material, so that they frequently lavish many days' labour on a piece of wood which is spoiled by knots or flaws.

No. 4576, a dagger, is another specimen of Stamboul or of Albanian coral and turquoise work.

No. 4375 is a Kurd ornament for the head in silver, studded with jade, coral, and turquoises; and No. 4377 is an Armenian belt of gilded brass with elaborate floral and strap work ornament.

No. 4378. A circular ornament of silver filigree, which was bought in Athens, is Byzantine, and serves to connect the Cuttack work with that of the Grecian Ionian Islands, of which it is also a speciality.

Nos. 4381 to 4383. A collection of small snuff gourds with incised ornament from Bokhara.

We now come to some more electrotypes, of which the principal are—

No. 4390. A Tazza, Italian, of the 16th century.

No. 4394. A Tazza bowl of Benvenuto Cellini from the Louvre in Paris. Subject: "The Triumph of Neptune."

No. 4391. Cast of a fibula, a kind of brooch, from the Royal Irish Academy in Dublin, and models of the Tara brooch (A.D. 800-900) of bronze, with appliques of gold and silver niello enamel and engraved and coloured glass.

Nos. 4397 to 4414. A clever series of reproductions (some in miniature) of ancient German arms and armour.

Lastly, the case contains many of the original brass astronomical instruments of Maharaja Sawai Jai Singh, the famous founder of Jeypore. These have been specially lent for exhibition by H. H. the Maharaja,

Case No. 161.

The recess cases in the centre room are all ornamented at the top with specimens of the cotton chintzes or dyed cloths, which are made at Sanganir, a town seven miles south of Jeypore, which stands on the bank of the Amanishah stream, whose waters are said to give the peculiar hue—the *couleur d'ivoire*—which is so much admired in many of these fabrics. The cloth is repeatedly washed in the river, the outlines of the patterns are applied from blocks in a kind of ink made of alum, turmeric, sulphate of iron, and madder, oil, etc., and the colours are applied by hand also from wooden blocks in the manner of a chromo-lithographic drawing. A few colours, *viz.*, black, red and pink only, are fast, while others fade after one or more washings. When the designs are printed on coarse country cloth or *rezi*, the effect is very bold and pleasing. In No. 4415 a favourite design of a poultry pigeon appears.

Below the chintzes are some examples of wooden tables (No. 4417), an overmantel (No. 4419), a Koran stand, which are painted in a peculiarly effective manner at Tilhar near Shahjehanpur in the North-West Provinces. This industry was revived and adapted to modern requirements by Mr. Muloch, C.S., the late Judge of Shahjehanpur. In the first instance, it was confined to the ornamentation of the *kishti* or tray in which wedding and durbar gifts are offered. The industry is suffering from the use of aniline pigments.

The case also contains a number of miscellaneous specimens of cane and grass work, for example a tray (No. 4430) from Bandar Abbas on the Persian Gulf, cane work (Nos. 4431, 4432) from the Thana Jail, grass mats (No. 4450) from Trichinopoly, a mat (No. 4438) made at Rewah from the bark of a date tree, etc.

Revolving Stand No. 162.

A series of frames attached to a central cylinder by hinges affords a very convenient and useful way of exhibiting drawings, etc.

On the top of the cylinder No. 162 is placed a fine copper Burmese bowl, 10 inches in diameter, which is supported on a stand composed of six griffins.

The following photographs are exhibited in the frames:—

Nos. 4461 to 4553. A series of the best specimens of industrial art work exhibited at the Lahore Exhibition of 1881-82.

Nos. 4554 to 4774. Photographs of the principal ancient buildings, and especially of the carved stonework on them, in Rajputana, Central India or Malwa, Bombay, Agra, Delhi, and the neighbourhood.

A careful study of these photographs, which are all by good artists, affords a most instructive insight into the richness and variety of decoration of a large number of the most interesting buildings in India.

Table No. 163.

In the centre of the room, opposite to the above stand, is an elegant table (No. 163), which was carved at Ahmedabad, and upon it is placed a very large marble fluted vase, with a high cover, which is carved with figures representing the Goddess of Fortune (Lakshmi or Shri), supported by elephants, who shower flowers upon her with their trunks.

PILLAR FRAMES No. 164.

These frames contain an interesting series of photographs of wood carving in Gujerat. Most of the old houses in Ahmedabad, and other large towns in that province, were enriched with magnificent wood carving. There is some doubt whether this beautiful art will flourish as much in the future as formerly. Some of the doors are remarkably fine. Mr. De Forest, a New York artist, is the main supporter of a most important wood-carving company at Ahmedabad, so, perhaps, we may hope that, as applied to the ornamentation of furniture, the art will yet flourish. Nos. 4822 to 4829 are examples of book binding from Ulwar, the only place in India in which this beautiful art is carried on to some degree of perfection. It is deteriorating in the hands of the descendants of the original artist. For further information the July number of the *Journal of Indian Art and Industry* for 1893 should be consulted.

CASE No. 165.

Carving on ivory dates from even prehistoric times, as specimens have been found in the cave-dwellings of the people who lived when the reindeer and mammoth inhabited Southern Europe (South Kensington Handbook). Examples are found in Egyptian tombs, and amongst the remains of old Assyrian palaces, while others have come down from Roman and Greek times.

The history of Roman and mediæval ivory carving is well illustrated by a series of reproductions by the Arundel Society, which will be found in the long case (No. 166) at the west end of this centre room. Some of the originals are very celebrated, as for example, Nos. 5076 and 5077. Two leaves of a diptych or a Roman writing table, on one of which are carved Æsculapius and Telesphorus, and on the other Hygeia and Cupid (probably of the 2nd century A.D.).

No. 5080. A leaf of a diptych of the 4th or 5th century, an angel with a globe, of a later date, is a specimen of the Greek School after the Emperor Justinian. Then come mirror cases of the mediæval period (13th and 14th centuries).

We now return to Case No. 165, in which will be found examples of nearly all kinds of ivory carving done in India at the present day.

On the whole, the best work probably now comes from Travancore and Murshidabad, but none of it equals the Burmese, and still less the elaborate work of the Chinese and Japanese.

There is however a clever Jeypore man, now serving in Udaipur, who carved three fine *burtanas* or turban-lifters (Nos. 5013 to 5015), which will be found in Case No. 166, above the Arundel Society's models, and also a fan of imitation palm leaves (No. 5020), which all show considerable skill in cutting ivory.

The cow (No. 4919) from Travancore is very well cut without the defects displayed in all the other representations of animals in the case.

A betelnut walking stick from the same place, with a portrait bust, which forms the handle, is very skilfully executed (No. 4851). It was made for the Dewan. In the centre of the case are, a model of Krishna playing the flute, from Jeypore, which won a prize at the Simla Exhibition of 1881 (No. 4864), and a perforated bouquet of flowers

(No. 4898) made at Patiala, where a short time ago a workman resided, who spent most of time in turning out very elaborate, though somewhat useless, work of this kind. Near it is a powder horn in the form of a mermaid, which is lent by H. H. the Maharaja of Jeypore (No. 4943). At the east end of the case are some finely plaited fans of ivory from Sylhet, each of which cost a large sum; but they are only examples of patient industry (Nos. 4967 and 4968). Perhaps the same may be said for the fly whisks or *chauries* of ivory threads from Bharatpur; but in the latter case the art of making the threads, which is known only to one or two families, renders them curious. The men are in the employ of the Maharaja of Bharatpur (see No. 6175 in Case No. 189).

The small minutely-worked hairpins from Mandalay (Nos. 4963, 4964, 4875 and 4880), models of a man and woman in gala dress from the same place, prove how much more cleverly the Burmese and other Eastern nations are in working in ivory than the Indians. Near these are a few Japanese figures and (Nos. 4921 to 4924) *netsukes* or belt toggles.

Some old ivory chessmen (No. 4899) from Jeypore, and (Nos. 4884 to 4896) grotesque bone figures from Surat, show more imagination than most of the modern Indian work.

Amongst the specimens from Murshidabad, the best are a representation (No. 4988) of the goddess Mahishasuri Devi or Durga, and a number of attendant gods and goddesses such as are represented at the Durga Puja in Bengal, and (No. 4843) a sporting elephant with attendants.

CASE No. 166.

This is the west large central case in the room, and, like the one on the east, it is chiefly filled with reproductions of European art, for the most part pottery, etc., which may be studied, in connection with similar collections of Indian ware in the end west room; of ancient ivories; and of miscellaneous articles of interest from different parts of the world. Amongst examples of Minton ware are:—

No. 5001. A porcelain vase (*pate sur pate*). Subject: A white figure of Cupid on a *blue celsete* ground. Artist: Mons. Solon, of Messrs. Minton & Co. A vase (No. 5002), and a small tile (No. 5032), reproductions of the famous Henri Deux or Oiron ware, which is unique of its kind, and very rare and costly. It has been said that "the forms are always pure in outline and in the style of the Renaissance, so that this exquisite pottery may be justly compared with the chased and damascened work of the 16th century." Only 80 pieces are supposed to exist, and none is a duplicate of another. Even reproductions are costly. A single drinking cup brought £1,100 at a sale in 1865.

Nos. 5025 to 5027, 5030, 5031 to 5033, 5034, 5035 to 5039. Specimens of painted tiles and saucers of different kinds and values.

No. 5029. A large tile or slab of porcelain by E. H. Marks, the painter of birds. Subject: One of the series called "The Seven Ages of Man."

No. 5040 is a large bowl, an example of Minton stone ware.

Nos. 5041 to 5075. A series of plaster casts of the best gems in the Berlin Museum. The subjects are mostly classical.

Nos. 5076 to 5390. A series of casts from ivory plaques selected from reproductions of the Arundel Society, London, to illustrate the history of ivory carving, and to enable comparisons to be made with the work of oriental artists in the adjoining case (No. 165). The principal examples are—

No. 5076. A Roman diptych of the 2nd century A. D. Subject: Æsculapius and Telesphorus.

No. 5077, Ditto. Subject: Hygeia and Cupid.

No. 5080, 4th or 5th leaf. Subjeet: An angel with a globe and sceptre.

Nos. 5082 to 5086. Byzantine work. Small plaques.

Nos. 5087 and 5088. Mediæval work. Subjects from the history of Joseph.

Nos. 5089 and 5090. Mirror case, 13th and 14th century. At the top and ends of the case are a number of artistic reproductions from the Ipsen Pottery Works in Denmark, and (No. 5004) a bronze Mercury copied from the original in the Loggia di Lanzi, Florence; busts of Homer (No. 5003), Diana à la Biche (No. 5018), Apollo Belvedere (No. 5016), Jupiter (No. 5011), Juno (No. 5009), the Venus of Milo (No. 5007), Achilles (No. 5006), Hermes after Praxitiles (No. 5005), two plaques by Thorwaldsen, Night (No. 5022), Morning (No. 5024), and two bas-reliefs by the same artist, *viz.*, Briseis leaving Achilles (No. 5023), and The Ages of Love (No. 5091).

Two Etruscan vases (Nos. 5012, 5008), a statue in terra cotta, The Dying Achilles, by Herther, a Grecian painted vase (No. 5017), and a Pompeian vase (No. 5019). Amongst the miscellaneous articles are the following:—

A Persian tray of mosaic in wood, gold, ivory, and mother-o'-pearl of the same character as the well-known Bombay inlay in Case No. 150. (No. 5092); leather boxes embroidered with needle-work from Bilaspur, a small hill state near Simla (Nos. 5094 and 5095); an ebony box of wood ornamented with ivory porcupine quills from Ceylon (No. 5101), a coffee table (No. 5099), and a Koran stand (No. 5112), with mosaic of mother-o'-pearl and ivory in the Constantinople style.

No. 5111. Model of a caique, the small boat which is used in the Golden Horn at Constantinople; an Albanian Darvesh stick of blackwood with brass wire inlay. This is shown because it is exactly like the work produced at Mainpuri in the N.-W. Provinces (see Case No. 150). It illustrates the difficulty of establishing the birthplace of any oriental art.

A carved ebony stick 200 years old; pipe and cigarette stems of various kinds; a carved steatite *hookah* from Kuteyah, near Broussa, Asia Minor (No. 5133); a carved Darvesh bowl formed of the half of a Seychelle Island cocoanut or Coco de Mer (No. 5131); and a Russian religious picture, which is shown here to illustrate the way in which the Byzantine School conventionalism soon fossilized art (No. 5132).

No. 10850. A Poppy plant is a well made model in ivory which was presented by H. H. the Maharaja of Benares (Case No. 256).

Pillar Frames No. 167.

All the frames on the pillar are filled with a most interesting series of photographs of the royal mummies and other objects which were found at Deir-el-Bahari, near Thebes, in 1881, by H. E. Brugsh Bey; also of a few places of interest in connection with them. The principal are as follow :—

Ras Kenen, King of Upper Egypt, about 1823 B.C., 17th Dynasty (No. 5136); side view of the head of Thotmes II, of the 18th Dynasty, 1073-1462 B.C. (No. 5142); four different photographs of Seti I, 19th Dynasty, 1462-1288 B.C. (Nos. 5143 to 5146); three of Rameses II, the Pharoah of the Oppression of the children of Israel, (Nos. 5147-5149), also of the 19th Dynasty; three of Rameses III of the 20th Dynasty, 1288-1110 B.C. (Nos. 5150 to 5152); the Princess, Nessi Khonson, 21st Dynasty, 1110 to 980 B.C. (Nos. 5153 to 5155); Queen Ameniritis, 25th Dynasty, 715-665 B.C. (No. 5168); the Great Sphinx at Gizeh, near Cairo (Nos. 5159 to 5163); the Pyramid of King Pepi I, 6th Dynasty, at Sakkara, 370 B.C.

The visitor should return to these photographs after examining the case of Egyptian antiquities in the adjoining corridor.

Case No. 168.

Kashmir papier-mâche work (much of which however is painted wood) has a very large sale in all Indian exhibitions. The art is clearly of Persian origin, many of the patterns being derived from that country; but others originated in the Happy Valley, especially the favourite ones, which are the same as those used on the Kashmir shawls.

Babu T. N. Mukerjee writes that Mr. Kipling states that "in response to the English demand for something chaste, the rich colouring and bold patterns formerly in vogue have given way to a somewhat sickly monochrome of cream colour and gold." This misfortune has not only happened to Kashmir work, but to many other art products in India, where colourists are becoming as timid as many of their European brethren. Amongst the numerous specimens in the case are :—

Nos. 5184, 5186, 5187, 5188. Four candlesticks, two of which are ornamented with flowers on a white ground, and two with the cone pattern found on shawls, which, according to some, is an imitation of the windings of the Jhelum river as seen from the top of the Takht-i-Suleiman hill, near Srinagar.

The mountain meadows or *margs*, studded over with flowers, suggest the many kinds of floral ornament, which are so profusely employed by the Kashmir artists. A water-bottle (No. 5189) is covered with figures of demons, rajas, and fairies. A pencase (such as Nos. 5192, 5201, 5205) is a purely native article; so also are the bedstead legs, shaped like birds. Book covers (Nos. 5194 to 5208, 5209), card boxes (No. 5198), trays (Nos. 5202 to 5204), bezique boxes (Nos. 5211 and 5213), cheroot cases (Nos. 5218-5219), jewel boxes (Nos. 5228 and 5230), and glove boxes (Nos. 5195 and 5198), are for European use.

More ambitious examples are a table with a backgammon board on the top (No. 5217) and a writing table (No. 5229).

A few large panels, to show the different designs and to serve as suggestions for the decoration of rooms, were especially prepared for the Museum (Nos. 523 5240, 5242, 5244, 5246, 5247). There are rooms in the palaces at Srinagar, the capital of Kashmir, the walls and ceilings of which are covered with such work. The remainder of the case is filled with examples of lacquer work—an art which will be noted at greater length in describing the contents of Case No. 180. At the top of the Case is a large cabinet from Bikanir in the west of Rajputana (No 5185). It is lacquered work, which is generally done on wood, but very frequently on pottery, glass, and even tin. A raised design is formed by means of liquid clay, which is applied with a squirrel-hair brush. The surface is then painted, and gold leaf is freely used over all. The effect is rich and good. The lacquered boxes with dome-shaped tops (Nos. 5190, 5191) and the nests of balls from Hyderabad in Sind (No. 5199), which are covered with hunting scenes in outline, delicately tinted on a rich brown ground, are really very beautiful. They are smoothly polished. Good examples are Nos. 5190, 5199. A rather well-finished box from Montgomery (No. 5193), a few articles from Patiala (No. 5241), a box and an elaborate toy from Sahiwal, in the Punjab, which is finished off with an ivory knob, and a pencase from Mozuffarnagar, complete the contents of the case.

CASE NO. 169.

The top of the case is filled with arms, which are arranged below a pair of Sanganir *chadars* or sheets, and a handsome mirror frame, and bracket of *shisham*, wood inlaid with ivory from Hoshiarpur in the Punjab (No 5250).

The *peshkabz* (No. 5254) is the common dagger used by all classes, particularly Mohamedans in North India.

The *chhora* or long knife is chiefly used in the Punjab (No. 5251).

The Afghan knife is still longer and very sharp (No. 5253).

The Nepalese use the *kukri*, a kind of bill which can be employed in cutting down jungle (No. 5262).

The *shamsher* (No. 5252) is the Persian long curved sword.

The *talwar* (No. 1272) is the Hindu sword—one of the national weapons. The specimen shown (No. 5265) has a serrated edge for cutting chain mail.

The Nagas, or religious monks of Jeypore, use a long gauntlet sword or *patta* of steel, which is called *dhu* (No. 5263). Fakirs and religious devotees carry about all sorts of curious weapons, as, for example (No. 5256), a sort of toasting fork with a handle formed of a deer's horn, and a parrying shield or *maru* (No. 5258), which has two antelope horns armed with steel points projecting from each side. Bows and arrows are still in use. Maces of curious form, many of them formerly well known in Europe, are found from time to time, such as the battle mace with a ball at the top covered with spikes, the holy water sprinkler of the mediæval bishops (No. 5260), and an axe shaped at the end like a hand which grasps a crowbill. Here also is a *gupti* or sword-stick (No. 5267). At the bottom of the cases are some quaint models of animals made of wood, which are painted and lacquered at Khandela in the Jeypore territory.

Lastly, there are grass shoes (Nos. 5274 to 5276), which are used throughout the Himalayas on the snows, and sandals made of the dwarf palm, which were bought in the Khaibar pass. Some mats and baskets from Peshawar cantonment are near them, and also a few fans of the khas-khas grass (*Andropogon muriaticus*) from Jeypore, Poona, and Sawantwadi, with bottles and boxes of the same from Kishengarh.

Case No. 173.

This case also contains arms. The following present points of interest :—

A small dagger with a walrus-ivory hilt. The *shirmahi* or walrus-ivory is much used in India for purposes of this kind (No. 5310). A sacrificial axe (*dhao*) with a Rajput hilt and knuckle guard with Assamese blade (No. 5312). Such combinations are common.

Below the arms are a few fans, grass baskets, etc., from the Seychelle Islands, and forty panels, each four inches square, showing all the ordinary Kashmir decorative designs as applied to papier-mâche ware. Some of them are very pretty (Nos. 5316 to 5355).

Recess Case No. 174.

Below two specimens of Sanganir chintz (Nos. 6369, 6370) showing the ivory ground, and a papier-mâche shield (No. 5371) ornamented with gilt figures, which is an example of a common Jeypore manufacture, are a number of weapons.

The straight sword or *khanda* is one of the national weapons of the Hindu (No. 5372). The *katār* or thrusting dagger near it is another (No. 5373). The *katār* is a dagger, with a triangular flattened blade, which is held in the hand by crossbars fastened between two long wrist guards. The flat surface of the blade is often chiselled into hunting or war pictures, and the bars are elaborately and richly damascened (Nos. 5374, 5375). The Mahratta steel mace (No. 5378) has two heads formed of cutting blades, which represent the divisions of the *kamrakh* fruit (*Averrhoa*). The plain battle axe (No. 5379) is termed a *tabar*. No. 5380 is a Bairagi or Hindu devotee's crutch, which he uses to lean upon. It contains a dagger, which can be drawn rapidly when the owner is in a sitting posture. Such a weapon is very characteristic of the men, and too often of their treacherous disposition, or of their dangerous lives in former times.

The mace with a globular end and spear point is Persian (No. 5382). The Mahratta crowbills (No. 5390, 5391) are powerful weapons.

No. 5392 is an Arab dagger or *jamaiya* with lunette-shaped hilt of ebony. Perhaps the most interesting of all is the *wagnak* (Vyághra Nakh) or steel tiger claws (No. 5395), such as Sivaji, the famous Mahratta chief, used for tearing open the abdomen of the Musalman General, Afsul Khan.

The bottom shelves are filled with lacquered boxes from Benares and Khandela in Jeypore (Nos. 5396 to 6405).

Case No. 180.

The case is filled with specimens of lacquered wood, which are ornamented in several different manners. The term "lac-turnery" has been thought the best for this kind of work, since the article is generally turned into round shapes and then covered with shellac, which is made to adhere and receive a high polish by rapid friction on the turner's frame. In some cases several layers of lac of different colours are applied, and the patterns are formed by cutting through one or more layers with a chisel according to the colour which it is required to expose. The ornament is sometimes mottled, an effect which is produced, according to Mr. Baden Powell, by using hard sticks of lac which are held lightly against the articles, so that only a point of colour here

5419 SCHOOL OF ART, JEYPORE.

5191 HYDERABAD, SIND.

5210 HOSHIARPUR.

5207 KASHMIR.

VIII. LACQUER WARE BOXES.

and there attaches itself. Flower patterns are produced with a fine chisel, which is used with extreme delicacy of touch by the workman. No one of the minor arts seems so universally practised as this is in the north of India, and especially in the Punjab, Sind, Rajputana, and the North-Western Provinces. One or two of the exhibits, which it has been most convenient to place in this case, are not shown as lacquered objects, but present special features of interest. For example, the terrestrial globe of Maharaja Sawai Jai Singh, the founder of Jeypore, the great astronomer, chief, and politician, who did so much to make the State famous in the days of the Emperor Mohamed Shah early in the 18th century. It was probably copied from an European original, and the names were written in Hindi by an Indian, as the globe accords with what was known of the world at that period. There are many maps and charts in the Jeypore palace, which were made in a similar way (No. 5414). A portable shrine (No. 5441) is placed at the south end of the case. It is very curious, and was bought from a travelling Brahman, who was using it at the time. There is a central shrine of Jagannath of Puri in Orissa. It has inner doors and outer ones, which are also shrines with folding doors, the whole forming a pentaptych. Every surface is covered with elaborate pictures, principally illustrating the mythology of the worshippers of Vishnu.

Nos. 5500, 5503 and 5506 are long elaborately painted and lacquered staves. They come from the private collection of the Maharaja, and are old and rare specimens. Nos. 5522, 5525 and 5526 are three maces (*chobs*), such as are carried by *chobdars* or superior peons or messengers. They are covered with wonderfully well drawn and painted figures of birds and animals or hunting scenes, enough, as an excellent authority once said, to start a school of design. These are lent by H. H. the Maharaja. The body of the case is filled with numerous specimens of smooth, brightly polished Benares lacquered boxes, toys, and small painted and quaint lacquered figures of animals from Jeypore and Khandela. These cost from four to five rupees per hundred. Vases, bottles, and boxes (Nos. 5418, 5419, 5429, 5430, 5431 and 5432) from the School of Art, Jeypore, which are decorated with etched animals, birds, etc., have been adapted from the maces above mentioned. Near them are boxes, etc., from Hoshiarpur, which is very celebrated for its smooth, mottled lacquer ware. Some of this work is further enriched with ivory discs, which are cut into different designs.

Nos. 5444 to 5454 are small, plainly lacquered articles, which came from Indargarh to the south of the Jeypore State. Lacquered pots are also made here, and have a considerable local reputation. Some of the variegated lacquer from Hyderabad in Sind is pretty, as, for example, the nests of boxes (Nos. 5467 and 5469), and balls (Nos. 5485 and 5487).

There are four glass bottles from Bikanir, which are elaborately ornamented with raised gilt diapers, and then lacquered. The circular panels from Agra are specimens of incised lacquer in which geometrical designs are cut out of layers of lac of different colours. The effect is hard and not pleasing (Nos. 5511, 5515, 5518 and 5523).

In the south-west corner of this room are a few articles, as for example—

No. 10849. A curious wooden and lacquered chair, ornamented with tigers in relief on the front legs and below the arms.

No. 5560. A carved black cabinet from Bombay.

No. 5559. A bracket of wood, covered with copper enamel, from Constantinople.

No. 5561. A model of a Nepalese man.

PILLAR FRAMES NO. 183.

We have here another set of photographs of Egyptian antiquities; in fact, the principal objects in the famous museum at Cairo. The most remarkable, where all are of surpassing interest, are perhaps the following:—The coffins of King Soquouri Tiouaquen who ruled at Thebes before 1703 B.C. (No. 5562); of Ahmos I, the conqueror of the Hyksos or Shepherd Kings, about 1703 B.C. (No. 5563); of Thotmos II (No. 5566); Seti I (No. 5568); and of Rameses II, or the Sesostris of the Greeks (No. 5569); the leather funeral tent of Queen Isimkheb (No. 5578); a crude basket containing the funeral repast of that princess (No. 5579); Jewels of the Queen Aah-hotep of the 18th Dynasty (Nos. 5594, 5595); the head of the wooden statue known as the Sheikh-el-Belled, of the 5th Dynasty, which ruled about 3951-3703 B.C. (No. 5598); head of King Menephta, the Pharoah of the Exodus (No. 5605); statue of King Chephren, builder of the second Pyramid, 4th Dynasty, 4235-3951 B.C. (No. 5608).

CASE NO. 184.

This case is devoted to glass-ware. In the centre of the front shelf is a circular panel of mosaic, from Salviati of Venice and London. Subject: The Head of St. Mark (No. 5628). A few vases and bowls from the same maker stand near it. Below them are seven specimens of old Persian glass (Nos. 5648 to 5651, 5635 to 5638), and some reproductions of Roman glass from Clautha, near Glasgow, in Scotland, which are exhibited because it is thought that similar ones could be made in Jeypore. Near them are one or two specimens of cameo glass, and plumes for the turban which were made in Udaipur from spun glass imported from Europe. Here are also two or three specimens of horn work from Ratnagiri in the Bombay Presidency (Nos. 5616 to 5618).

PILLAR FRAMES NO. 185.

These contain specimens of painting on talc, and painted leather mats from Trichinopoly (Nos. 5718 to 5723), and pieces of embroidered trimmings in China silk, which illustrate the debased results of the use of aniline dyes (Nos. 5715 to 5809).

A few other pieces from Delhi, Ulwar, and Lucknow near them are less injured. Some specimens of embroidery by Parsi women, done with Chinese silk in chain stitch, and a few of Chinese embroidery, are also shown, as well as many pieces of machine-made embroidery from Surat.

RECESS CASE NO. 186.

This large side case is chiefly filled with basket and mat work; but there are a few weapons, such as Nos. 5819 to 5822, the spears used by the Vedas, a very wild aboriginal tribe of Ceylon. Close by are some small tables from Shahjehanpur, ornamented in the style already noticed, and an octagonal carved wooden Turkish table, the top of which is formed of Turkish tiles (No. 5885). It was purchased in Constantinople.

STAND OF REVOLVING FRAMES NO. 187.

The frames on this stand are chiefly devoted to illustrations in colour of various art books (Nos. 5886 to 6095).

A series of 33 prints illustrating the mode of reproducing paintings by chromo-lithography—subject: "The Emperor Jehangir giving audience at Ajmere"—from the Memorials of the Jeypore Exhibition, by the author of this handbook. Published by Mr. Griggs, of Peckham, London (Nos. 5886 to 5918).

Several illustrations from the same work are shown (Nos. 5919 to 5927) as examples of high-class chromo-lithography, as well as a *fac-simile* of a Charter of Richard III of England (No. 5928); and also the principal plates from Messrs. Audsley and Bowes' great work on the Keramic arts of Japan (Nos. 5929 to 5948). Next to these are some native paintings of the best class (Nos. 5949 to 5988). They are followed by illustrations from the South Kensington Portfolios of Art, chiefly of specimens of Oriental Industrial Art (Nos. 6006 to 6050), and photographs and drawings from valuable works, which were given in exchange by the German Government for copies of the Memorials of the Jeypore Exhibition, which were presented to them by H. H. the Maharaja of Jeypore (Nos. 6051 to 6062), *e. g.*:—

Selection from a work on the marriage gifts to the Empress Frederick. German wood-carving (Nos. 6051 to 6062). Twelve coloured designs of Persian carpets from a work by Mr. Vincent Robinson, C.I.E. (Nos. 6003 to 6704).

Another set of Indian paintings (Nos. 6075 to 6095).

The pedestal of the stand is surmounted by a Burmese copper bowl on a support formed of griffins.

PILLAR FRAMES NO. 188.

(PAINTINGS.)

The subject of native painting is a very wide one, and the whole of the collections on the ground floor really serve to illustrate it, because in every case in which an object is to be made, a design is almost always prepared in the first place, and, where the beauty of the specimen depends upon the surface decoration, the artist works directly upon it. It is a matter of indifference to him whether he paints on ivory, paper, wood, tin, talc, or on the plaster of a house-wall; whether he produces a miniature or decorates a palace front or a piece of pottery.

The frames before us are, however, devoted chiefly to portraits, and especially to the more common kinds which are sold in the bazárs. They are generally done on cards with Indian local colours and Chinese white; but, to save the trouble of preparing his pigments in the good old way, as mediæval European artists also used to do, the Jeypore man usually contents himself in these days with using the cheaper English paint boxes which are sold in the shops. In the collection are shown examples of his skill from the worst to the best. Sets of portraits of chiefs and nobles, which are usually traditional, and conventional likenesses are made.

Thus we have (Nos. 6096 to 6110) a set of portraits of the Chiefs of Jeypore from Maharaja Prithwi Singh, A.D. 1548, to Maharaja Sawai Ram Singh, A.D. 1880. Each

Prince is distinguished by holding in his hand a rose, a sword, a hawk, or something which is supposed to indicate his character.

Nos. 6105 to 6110 are small copies of what are supposed to be contemporary portraits which are now in the palace at Jeypore, and are more carefully executed than the others.

Paintings of gods, shrines, etc., are very common. The favourite subjects are—Ganesha, God of Wisdom (No. 6119); Hanuman, the Monkey-God (No. 6115); Ramachandra (an incarnation of Vishnu), the deified King of Oudh (Ajudhya), and Sita, his wife (Nos. 6120, 6122, 6125); Krishna, the Apollo of India, the great incarnation of Vishnu (Nos. 6118, 6121, 6123, 6135, 6138 to 6140); the goddess Devi or Durga, Kali or Parvati (Nos. 6127 to 6132), the wife of Shiva; the incarnations of Vishnu, the second member of the Hindu Trimurti or Trinity, and of Shiva, the third member (No. 6142); a series showing men and women at the toilet or amusing themselves (Nos. 6143 to 6150); and sporting subjects, such as (No. 6152) a Rajput spearing a tiger, etc.

CASE NO. 189.

A few choice articles have been arranged in this case. Amongst them are thirty carved and painted wooden figures representing most of the Burmese occupations and professions (Nos. 6153 to 6174). A fine old red coral lac box from Suchow in China. It is very delicately carved in the best manner (No. 6182).

H. H. the Maharaja of Mysore presented a walking stick inlaid with ivory (No. 6191).

Two beautiful fly whisks or *chauris* of sandalwood with elaborately carved handles and threads of very fine hair of the same (Nos. 6189 and 6190).

Close to it there is an ivory *chauri* from Bharatpur (No. 6175).

There are several specimens of Japanese tortoiseshell ware. No. 6192 is a model of a palanquin, No. 6180 of a jinriksha or chair drawn by a man, and No. 6181 the model of a junk or boat. Then comes a dressed model of a Chinese porter carrying water-pots suspended from a pole (No. 6176), of another carrying fowls (No. 6193), of a Japanese house (Nos. 6194), some carved stag horn work from Ratnagiri, shell bracelets from Dacca, and a Burmese manuscript from Mandalay.

CASE NO. 190.

It is of course impossible to obtain the best examples that have been produced of every industrial art which is practised in India; but photographs and drawings are available in most cases, and, with the help of other valuable specimens in the Museum, it is now easy, not only for the visitor to study the arts themselves very thoroughly, but, in most cases, to have reproductions made of the finest examples, because Jeypore workmen can copy almost anything of an oriental character with great success.

Exhibitions present good opportunities of making collections such as have been described, and the series shown in the set of pillar frames Nos. 6216 to 6271 are selections from the best of them. They were prepared at the close of the Simla Exhibition of 1881. Many of the objects obtained prizes. The following classes are exhibited :—Ivory carving, enamel on gold and silver jewellery, lacquer on wood, Moradabad ware, Persian pierced metal work, damascening in gold and silver, lacquered and enamelled copper and plated copper, book binding, and Burmese wood carving.

CASE NO. 192.

The south-east angle of the room forms a little Burmese court. Near the window, which looks into the back gallery of the Museum, are plaster casts of a Burmese man and woman of respectable position, clothed in the characteristic dress of the country. Above them are two deeply undercut carved frames and doors or windows. They are copied from originals in the king's palace at Mandalay, the capital of Burma (Nos. 6272, 6275, or 191, 193).

The large case contains numerous specimens of wood carving and of lacquer work, with some examples of figures or marionettes in cloth, and a few miscellaneous articles. The wall or recess case is for the most part filled with lacquer.

Mr. Tilly considers that the chief characteristics of the Burmese architectural carving are delicacy of its curves, the skill with which figures of birds and animals, or even men, are introduced, and the care with which every detail, however rough it may be, is worked out in strict accordance with truth and the propriety of art.

The skilful undercutting and the boldness of the designs are remarkable. There is no mistaking the influence of the Chinese on the Burmese workman, not only in the wood carving, but in all branches of art. The figures are very cleverly done, especially the small ones in the round of men and women of different ages and occupations, as, for example, a group of football players (Nos. 6294 to 6299), two actresses (Nos. 6303, 6304), soldiers (Nos. 6308, 6309), beggars (Nos. 6310, 6311), a female figure wearing a silk loin cloth (*temain*), the usual dress of women; a very good specimen (No. 6316), all in sandal-wood.

There are also other figures in a soft white wood (Nos. 6334 to 6341), and some in painted wood, chiefly of demons (Nos. 6322 to 6328).

The models of vehicles are interesting, as for example (Nos. 6317, 6345), common country carts with bullocks, and (No. 6285) a covered carriage also drawn by bullocks.

No. 6302 is a *belan* or demon holding a triangular brass gong. The wooden elephant, with ivory tusks (No. 6314), is a faithful representation of that clever animal; and No. 6315 is a wall bracket supported by three female figures, the whole being cleverly cut out of one piece of white wood. The price, Rs. 15, was very low.

The lacquered ware of Burma is well known. Mr. Tilly writes that it is of two kinds—

(1) Basket work lacquered over.

(2) Lacquered wood.

The former comes from Upper Burma; the latter chiefly from Lower Burma.

Amongst the wooden articles are platters in which a family dinner is served (Nos. 6391, 6392), round and square boxes (Nos. 6375, 6384), and bowls (Nos. 6365 to 6369), bowls with pagoda-shaped covers used for carrying food to the monasteries, pagodas, and shrines, or on which to place images of Gautama Buddha (No. 6333).

Coffers are made in black and gold for holding palm-leaf manuscripts (Nos. 6415 and 6416).

Tables in black and gold are also made. These are covered with elaborate drawings. No. 6401 is a good example.

There are in our collections several fine panels of lac in black and gold, and others in bas-relief. The latter are very cleverly executed.

The case contains also a few marionettes or small figures which are worked by the fingers of the performer and with string, in the same manner as in the well-known Punch-and-Judy shows of England (Nos. 6282, 6289, 6343 and 6344).

Some curious glass ear-rings from the Shan Country show how far human beings will torment themselves when ornament is concerned. The perforation of the lobe of the ear in this case is large enough to hold a cylinder three-fifths of an inch in diameter. Some wax ornaments for the hair (Nos. 6287, 6312) are also very curious.

Attention should be given to the rice-cups, cylindrical boxes for turbans, etc., many of which fit into each other, the large gilt folding umbrella (No. 6332) (the King of Burma was the "Lord of the Umbrella," it will be remembered), and the paper fan (No. 6342).

WALL CASE NO. 197.

This case contains for the most part Burmese lacquer boxes and a few specimens of arms from Jeypore. They are exhibited only as decorative examples, being of no great value. Large quantities of weapons of all kinds, but generally of fantastic shape, are made in Jeypore for the special use of the tourist, who uses them to decorate his rooms in Europe, and to serve as memorials of his travels.

No. 6273 is a blackwood book stand from Ahmedabad. It is a fair specimen of furniture, which, until quite recently, was in great demand on the western side of India. The style shows Portuguese influence. The art furniture, which is now made in Bombay, has taken the place of the older manufacture to a great extent in Anglo-Indian houses. On the top of the shelf of the stand has been placed a Burmese musical instrument—a *patala* or harmonicon.

CHAPTER VI.

SOUTH CORRIDOR.

REVOLVING FRAMES NO. 198.

These frames contain textiles as follows :—

Nos. 6525 to 6538. A set of Japanese cotton prints of great variety.

Nos. 6586 to 6604. Burmese silk waist (*temain*) cloths worn by both men and women, of pleasing designs and combinations of colours.

Nos. 6605 to 6675. Specimens of cotton lace made in Kandi in Ceylon.

Nos. 6587 to 6589. Cotton waist cloths from Burmah.

Nos. 6578 to 6580. Embroidery from Lucknow.

Nos. 6565 to 6570. Embroidered muslin from Trichinopoly.

No. 6560. Lace made by Christian girls at Nazareth, Tinnevelly.

Nos. 6557 to 6558. Cotton coloured cloths from Trichinopoly.

Nos. 6551 to 6555. Bags embroidered in silk and gold thread from Madura; they are used for carrying sacred ashes.

No. 6549. A piece of embroidery and painting on silk from Japan—a delicate combination of two styles of work.

No. 6540. Borders of gold thread and beetle wing embroidery from Trichinopoly.

UPRIGHT CASE NO. 199.

This contains some specimens of garnet jewellery of the best workmanship.

REVOLVING SET OF FRAMES NO. 200.

The whole of the thirty frames are filled with specimens of machine-made lace of all the kinds which are made in Nottingham. They were presented by the Corporation of that town in exchange for gifts of models by H. H. the Maharaja of Jeypore.

FRAME NO. 205.

A plate, showing ancient and modern arms and armour with a description.

No. 104, of the Bouasse Lebel Series, Paris.

UPRIGHT CASE NO. 206.

This contains necklaces of garnets, and carbuncles, of moonstone (Nos. 7051 and 705), Lapis lazuli (No. 7061), and of crystal beads (Nos. 7054 and 7060).

SET OF REVOLVING FRAMES NO. 207.

The frames are chiefly filled with paintings and photographs.

No. 7065. Outline sketch of Krishna and female attendants in a garden, delicately drawn.

No. 7067. Water colour, Saraswati, the goddess of learning, shows European influence.

No. 7068. Water colours, a native beauty at her toilet.

Nos. 7059 to 7160. Photographs of buildings and places of interest in the Jeypore State and Capital, and at Ajmere. The latter were presented by the Local Government. Many of the views are tinted to give an idea of the colouring of the stone, &c. Nos. 7161 to 7166 are specimens of Persian caligraphy and illuminations by Mir Zaki.

Large Upright Frame No. 212.

This frame is filled with a collection of specimens of silk from Thana in the Bombay Presidency, which were presented in exchange by the Government of Bombay.

Large Upright Frame No. 213.

This frame is filled with selected examples of coloured chintzes from Sanganir. They are printed on English cloth.

Revolving Frames No. 214.

Nos. 7305 to 7329. Mixed cotton and silk cloths for the corsets of women from South India.

Nos. 7330 to 7341. A series of silk cloths used for the same purpose in Surat.

Nos. 7342 to 7353. A set of the same from Poona.

Nos. 7354 to 7371. A set from the Central Provinces.

Twenty-four specimens of Thana silk.

Nos. 7580 to 7583. Cloths for corsets from Ujjain and Sholapur.

Upright Case No. 221.

On the upper shelves in the case are shown some specimens of translucent enamel from Christiania in Norway (Nos. 7592 to 7597). They are made of parcel gilt silver wire, in the interstices of which clear enamels of bright colours are set, giving the appearance of beautiful gems in outlines of gold.

Amongst them are:—No. 7592. A dessert spoon. No. 7594. An oval dish. No. 7597. A salt cellar and a number of spoons.

Mr. C. Purdon Clarke, Keeper of the Art Collections, South Kensington Museum, thinks they will serve to afford useful hints to the Jeypore Enamellers.

The lower shelves are filled with bronze paper weights in the form of human figures, and ash trays, and a paper knife from Japan (Nos. 7598 to 7609).

Revolving Frames No. 224.

These Frames contain Textiles.

Nos. 7612 to 15 show, in a series of prints on the cloth, the mode of preparing the stamped cloths such as those that are made at Sanganir and Agra. The process is very similar to that employed in chromo-lithography.

Nos. 7616 to 7678. Cotton prints from Agra and Mathura. The former are used for floor cloths or *jazims*, the latter for petticoats of women.

Nos. 7629 to 7632. Coarse chintzes from Karauli.

After these come a series of cloths dyed with fugitive colours from Jeypore (Nos. 7660 to 7683).

Fugitive dyes are much used in Rajputana, as the people wear different coloured cloths at different seasons or festivals, and find it cheaper to re-dye the same cloth, over again and again, than to purchase, or keep fabrics dyed with permanent pigments for all the different occasions.

It is for these purposes that aniline dyes find such a ready sale.

Nos. 7684 to 7696. Pieces of coarse cloth rudely embroidered with diapers and borders by peasant women. Some of them are set with round bits of looking glass. This kind of work is considered to be very ancient. The cloths are used as borders for veils and petticoats.

Nos. 7703 to 7706. Coarse cloths for women's petticoats from Jeypore.

Nos. 7708 to 7713. A piece of cloth stamped with different colours to show the process of printing Sanganir chintzes.

Nos. 7714 to 7721. Coarse cloths from Kishangarh, and Nos. 7722 to 7734 from Ajmere. The two are practically the same, because a Kishangarh dyer made the latter while an inmate of the Ajmere Jail. The designs used by this man, especially for the borders, are very good.

Nos. 7735 to 7738. Coarse cloths from Bagru, which are very like those made at Sanganir.

Nos. 7739 to 7742. Cloths from Jeypore and Ajmere, in which the ground is covered with diaper and other designs in base metal either to imitate gold or silver.

Nos. 225 and 227. Carved wooden panels with a projecting balcony supported on a bracket and with a semi-dome above. They are made at Amritsar.

FRAMES NOS. 229 AND 231.

Two frames of casts from the British Museum of engraved stones, *viz.*:—

No. 229. Archaic Greek Island and Phœnician gems, Etruscan Scarabs, and early Greek gems.

No. 231. Later Greek and Græco-Roman gems.

UPRIGHT CASE NO. 230.

On the three upper shelves are a set of Pehlvi seals, which were found in Seistan, Central Asia, and purchased at Peshawar (Nos. 7894 to 7907).

No. 7908 is a Grecian intaglio seal found in Kabul. Subject: A man before a Hermes.

In the lower part of the case are eight small Burmese finger bowls (Nos. 7911 to 7915).

Nos. 236 and 237. These frames contain specimens of Japanese embroidery, and in No. 238 are some pieces of old Persian velvet, and in No. 239 Bulgarian embroidery made in Constantinople by women who were in exile.

Frames Nos. 240 to 242, and 250 to 255 contain specimens of embroidery from different places, and Frames Nos. 243 to 245, 247, 248 and 249, specimens of old Persian and Turkish tiles and a salver from Multan.

CASE NO. 256.

This case contains specimens of Jeypore and Bikanir pottery for the Imperial Institute; also materials and tools which are used in the manufacture of pottery.

WEST CORRIDOR, SHOW CASE NO. 257.

This case is chiefly devoted to porcelain and non-Indian pottery. It is well known that there is no indigenous porcelain, but, from time to time, a good deal of Persian, Chinese and Japanese ware has found its way into India, and has been much valued by the Moghul and other great Musalman families. Valuable pieces are occasionally fonnd in Delhi, Agra, Burhanpore, and other Musalman capitals, though not so frequently as formerly. Most of our specimens came from Delhi. Nos. 8139 to 8141, and 8163, 8164, 8170, 8172, 8179, 8190, are specimens of Nankin blue (Chinese) vessels. No. 8142 is a white wine bottle in the shape of a junk from Japan. A vase, shaped like a Hindu devotee's water-gourd, is a specimen of white crackle China or Celadon (No. 8158). No. 8173 is a large vase with black dragons in relief on the bowl. It is a modern specimen of white crackle China.

In the bottom of the case are numerous pieces of Celadon Porcelain, so called from a French hero of romance. The Indian dealers term it Ghori Porcelain. It is said to have been presented in large quantities to the Delhi Emperors by the East India Company, because it was found that the emperors valued it on account of the idea that it was supposed to crack if poisoned food were put into it, hence the accumulation of so many bowls or plates. It is of a very dark green colour, and is often crackled under the glaze. There are many different designs or marks under the glaze also, which are characteristic of different periods. Most of it was made, it is said, at King-te-Ching as far back as the thirteenth century. No. 8175 is a plate with a fluted margin and acanthus-like leaves in the centre. Nos. 8181 and 8182 are similar, but have fish-like marks. No. 8186 has the chrysanthemum flower. No. 8194 has two fish; and No. 8196, six large leaves. Nos. 8184, 8188 and 8189 are deep large bowls with shrub-like marks, and No. 8191 is a fine jar.

There are eleven specimens of pottery on a cream-coloured ground enriched with conventional flowers in red and blue with a fine glaze from Kuteya, near Broussa, in Asia Minor. The forms are artistic (Nos. 8143 to 8153). Near them are eight specimens of glazed pottery from Arjamothan in Persia, which are about 90 or 100 years old.

The ground is generally a dark blue, and the ornaments are flowers and figures (Nos. 8154 to 8161).

No. 8166 is rather a fine Persian basin of blue and white porcelain, and No. 8167 an ewer for the same with brass mounts. They are 170 years old.

Nos. 8168 and 8169 are two specimens of Japanese Imari ware. Nos. 8165 and 8173 are two large double gourd-shaped Japanese vases of modern manufacture. No. 8181 is a waterpot of green, yellow, and red pottery, with arabesque ornament from Milas, near Ismid, in Anatolia, Asia Minor; and No. 8184, a flower vase from Taragham, in Persia. Both were bought in Constantinople.

On the walls near Case No. 257 are a few specimens of tiles, &c.

No. 8053 (243) is an old Persian tile.

No. 8054 (244) is modern Persian.

No. 8055 (245) is also old Persian.

Nos. 8059 (248) and 8060 (249) are Turkish tiles from Constantinople.

Near the walls are some other interesting objects, as, for example, a cabinet of ivory inlay on sheesham wood from Hoshiarpur in the Punjab, which illustrates the judicious application of ivory to the ornamentation of furniture (No. 8063). A large carved teakwood almirah (*armoire*), the Indian name for a wardrobe. It was made by Messrs. Maggan Bhai Hatti Singh of Ahmedabad (Nos. 8045 and 8046). Two Japanese cabinets, illustrating the artistic treatment of beautifully grained woods (No. 8047), embroidery in gold and silver on silk (Turkish).

No. 8047. Persian figured velvet.

A very large and fine piece of embroidery by Bulgarian women in Constantinople Subject: Ramses III driving a chariot.

CHAPTER VII.

POTTERY ROOM.

The third great hall on the ground floor of the Museum has been termed the Pottery Room, because most of the cases contain collections, which are intended to illustrate the potter's art.

CASE NO. 258.

The upper shelves are filled with Bikanir pottery, which is divided into two classes, *viz.* :—

I. That which has raised decoration in colour and gold. It has been described when treating of its application to wood (page 64); and

II. A series with flat painted ornament in colour and gold.

Common red clay pots are generally used by the artist, but, in order to ensure better results, large quantity of vessels in white clay were made at Jeypore in the School of Art, and then sent to Bikanir for completion. Most of the forms selected are purely oriental, but some are Greek. The best examples of the first class are Nos. 8229, 8237, 8241, 8243, 8245, 8258, 8274 and 8280; of the second class, Nos. 8202, 8210, 8217, 8242, 8250, 8275, 8277, and 8282. In front of the case are some specimens from Delhi of white semi-translucent pottery with a strong glaze, which is decorated in white and blue. The ware is the same as that made in Jeypore, but is somewhat more vitreous, and less white. The first potter in Jeypore came from Delhi and introduced his art. His materials were rather better than those of his relations who remained at Delhi, hence his productions are more perfect and pleasing. A full description of the manufacture will be found at page 84.

No. 8228 is a preserve jar.

Nos. 8288 to 8298 are jars and boxes of different shapes.

The Multan pottery, of which No. 8201 is an example, has also a good white glaze with blue floral ornament, but the basis is a red clay; the colouring is much darker, and the designs are more varied than in the Delhi ware. A white saline efflorescence is often noticed after a short time on the vessels, which, moreover, are too porous to serve for holding fluids. Their bright and pure colouring however render them very decorative. The Delhi and Jeypore ware has a colder effect. Several interesting specimens of pottery came from Bulandshahr, where Mr. Growse found a man who was at work in quite a new style. Here again the base is pottery. The ornament is in brown white and blue colours, and some of it is in the form of tracery, as, for example, No. 8219, a large flat vase. In No. 8257 the glaze is dark blue in colour. Somewhat similar ware is made at Burhanpur, the former Moghul capital of the Central Provinces, a city which was on the great highway from the West Coast to Hindustan, that is to say, the country between the Jamna and Ganges, which was the seat of empire under the Moghul Emperors. No. 8259 is a plate, and No. 8262 a teapot. The base is red glaze pottery, and the colours of the ornament are yellow, green, and brown. Red, white, and blue pottery is also made at Rampore in the North West Provinces (No. 8283 a gourd-shaped lota or waterpot, and No. 8287 a jar). The Khurja pottery, also from the N. W. P., has white and blue floral ornament, otherwise it resembles the Rampore work. The most interesting however is the ware from Jalandhar

9336

9209

9206

9185

8422

8403

8366

8248

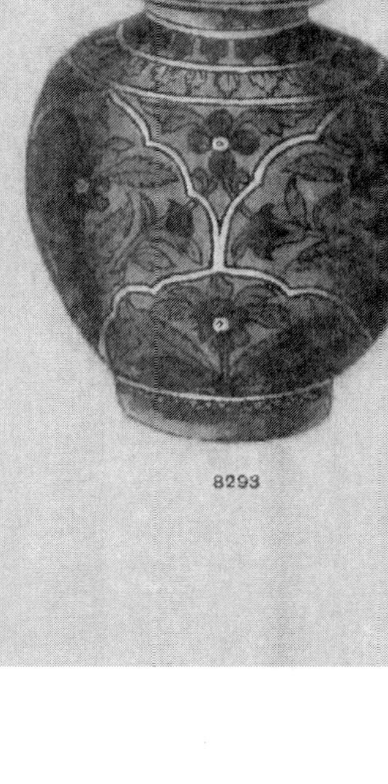
8293

9336 WATER BOTTLE. JEYPORE
9209 VASE: 9206 VASE; 9185 VASE.
ALL AMBER PATTERNS MADE AT JEYPORE.
8422 BULANDSHAHR.

8403 PILGRIM FLASK. MULTAN.
8366 WATER BOTTLE. PESHAWAR.
8248 OIL VESSEL. BIKANIR.
8293 WATER POT. DELHI.

IX. POTTERY.

in the Punjab, which is made by a Musalman, one Mohamed Sharif, who is acquainted with the art of manufacturing such tiles as those which were used to ornament many of the palaces and tombs, that were constructed in the times of the Emperors Jehangir and Aurangzeb at Lahore and elsewhere. The ornament is formed of small slips or appliques of different colours, which are very bright and pure. It is a kind of *pate-sur-pate* work. The old man used to turn out beautiful panels of flowers (see No. 265 on the wall of this room adjoining the case), but, finding it did not pay so well as the manufacture of common plates and dishes for the Commissariat Department, he can now hardly be induced to produce any specimens at all. One or two pieces that he showed at the Lahore Exhibition of 1894, are very inferior to those produced a few years ago.

Amongst the examples in the case are blue white and red tiles (Nos. 8300 and 8304), and two fruit dishes (Nos. 8301 and 8302).

A waterpot or *barni* of clay, with an elaborate design of carved arabesques, which are painted and gilded, is very curious. It came from the Bombay Presidency and is a *tour de force* of some genius in a country village.

Specimens of such local talent are to be found at most exhibitions in India.

RECESS CASE NO. 259.

(PESHAWAR WARE.)

The tops of all the recess cases in the room have a pair of Sanganir chintz cloths, which are ranged for decorative purposes as well as to show the endless varieties of a local manufacture.

Immediately below the chintzes are seven small tiles placed in the form of a star. They were made at Jalandhar.

Scattered through the case are a number of specimens of Peshawar pottery, a kind of coarse majolica of clay with richly glazed splashes of green, yellow, and brown colours by way of ornament (Nos. 8350 to 8366).

Most of the shapes are European, and some are grotesque, as, for example, No. 8359, a water-bottle ornamented with tigers' heads.

At Bahawalpur, the capital of a Mohamedan State of the same name, near Multan, in the Punjab, a delicate very light brown kind of pottery is made. Some of it is perforated (Nos. 8339 and 8349), and some lobed (Nos. 8340 to 8343 and 8384 to 8349). It is ornamented in some cases with fine black outlines.

WALL FRAMES NOS. 260 TO 265.

No. 8367 (260) is the first of a series of wall frames which contain pieces of velvet ornamented with Indian patterns. They were presented by Mr. T. Wardle, of Leek, President of the Silk Association of Great Britain, who has done so much to advance our silk manufactures, and especially to increase the popularity of Indian designs, and to improve and promote production of raw silk in India.

It was decided to show all the examples in this room, so that they might be seen to the best advantage.

No. 8373 (263) is a piece of cotton, which was also made and decorated with an Indian design at Leek.

Nos. 8368 to 8371 (261). Four plaques showing the different modes of decorating wall surfaces in fresco and distemper, etc., in use in Jeypore. They were made under the supervision of Col. Jacob, C.I.E., Superintending Engineer of the State.

No. 8372 (262) is a large Persian brick or tile of modern manufacture. It is glazed and ornamented with a picture of a feast.

Nos. 8374 (264) and 8375 (265). Tiles by Mohamed Sharif of Jalandhar. No. 8375 is a large panel made in two pieces, and is an excellent example of the *pate-sur-pate* work already referred to.

RECESS CASE NO. 266.

(MULTAN POTTERY.)

Nearly the whole of this case is filled with Multan pottery.

Plates with a great variety of ornament are shown of all sizes, also vases and jars. The collection illustrates the facility of the artist in decorative treatment, and especially the ease with which he conventionalizes floral forms. The process of manufacture has already been described. Tiles for the enrichment of tombs and other buildings were in all probability the first forms in which the ware was produced. Large chimney pieces are now made of this ware. It is however somewhat brittle. There are a few specimens of Bulandshahr pottery on the lower shelf in the case (Nos. 8416, 8420 and 8422).

WALL FRAME NO. 268.

It contains a reproduction, on rather a smaller scale, in the School of Art, Jeypore, of an illustration (No. 8426) from L'Art Arabe by Prisse d'Avennes. It represents the Kaaba at Mecca with its surroundings, and is composed of sixty-three small separate panels of the semivitreous pottery of Jeypore.

In the revolving pillar frames No. 269 close by are a few small Multan tiles, a pair of book covers of Bikanir raised work in gold and colour, and not far off are two well made casts of a man and woman from the Andaman Islands, who attended at the Calcutta Exhibition of 1883.

JAPANESE POTTERY NO. 270.

In accordance with the plan adopted in other rooms, a few specimens of oriental ware from China, Japan, Turkey, etc., have been collected, and some examples of English and Hungarian porcelain and pottery, of no great intrinsic value, but simply to serve as examples for the use of students. Case No. 270 contains an assortment of Japanese porcelain and pottery from Kaga (Nos. 8465 to 8471), Hizen (Nos. 8466 to 8470), and Satsuma (Nos. 8467 and 8468).

Some of the common plates from Kioto are also shown (Nos. 8493 to 8497).

No. 8502 is an old painted and gilt porcelain tray. The place of manufacture is unknown. The names given above are those of different Japanese provinces or towns after which the ware is named.

Case No. 271.

This case contains specimens of Hungarian porcelain, which are exhibited on account of the beauty of the colouring and the oriental forms of the vessels. The Hungarians are reputed to be of oriental origin, and pride themselves upon their power of adopting oriental art ideas, hence their work ought to be peculiarly instructive in an eastern museum. It is unnecessary to describe the different examples. On one of the shelves will be found portions of a tea set of blue and white porcelain, which were bought in the Peshawar bázar as specimens of Russian manufacture (Nos. 8507 to 8506 and 8513 to 8515). Some time ago, it is said that certain Moscow dealers exported a good deal of this ware to Central Asia, but, not being able to meet the demand, they obtained a specially prepared supply from England, which they continued to send out as Russian work to their old markets (Nos. 8507 to 8509 and 8513 to 85:5).

Pillar Frames No. 272.

The revolving frames attached to the adjacent pillar No. 272 are filled with a most interesting series of lacquered panels, on which are painted a number of the symbols that are used in India.

In fact, they may be said to represent Indian symbolism. The following are the subjects :—

No. 8532. The twelve signs of the Zodiac.
No. 8533. The regents of the ten quarters.
No. 8534. The three divisions of the day.
No. 8535. The twelve months personified.
Nos. 8536 and 8537. The thirty-six modes of music.
Nos. 8538 and 8539. The twenty-four Jain Lords or Tirthankaras.
Nos. 8540, 8541. The goddesses of the twenty-four Jain Lords.
No. 8544. The Jain worlds, Past, Present, and Future.
No. 8546. The ten forms of the Goddess Devi.
No. 8547. }
No. 8549. } The Insignia of Royalty.
No. 8550. }
No. 8548. The eight ominous things kept ready by the God Indra on the birth of a Jain Lord.
Nos. 8551 and 8552. The sixteen evil dreams of Raja Chandra Gupta.
Nos. 8553 and 8554. The sixteen dreams of a Jain god's mother.
Nos. 8555 and 8556. The symbols of the twenty-four Jain Lords.
Nos. 8559 to 8563. The signs of the twenty-eight lunar asterisms.
No. 8564. The nine planets. Next come some Jain stories illustrated on panels, as follow :—

No. 8542. A story of the uncertain tenure of the pleasures of the world and the dangers thereof.

No 8543. The virtue of different men illustrated by the way they gather the fruit of a mangoe-tree. The black or wicked man cuts off a branch or even the tree down altogether. The good, or white man, only picks up the fallen mangoes.

No. 8545. Birth of the first Jain Lord. A few panels are copied from the Razmnamah of the Emperor Akbar and are shewn here, *e.g.* :—

No. 8557. The imminent peril of Indra, King of Heaven.

No. 8558. The ordeal of Sita.

No. 8559. Death of Rama's generals.

No. 8560. Krishna killing Kansa, the Hindu Herod.

No. 8561. The Great Horse Sacrifice of the Pandava brothers.

No. 8562. The marriage choice ceremony of Nala and Damayanti.

NICHE CASE NO. 275.

(SIND POTTERY.)

The whole of this case is filled with cheap pottery from Hala in Sind. The patterns are bold, and the colours employed are bright and striking.

The collection is shown, in connection with the better known, and more magnificent, examples, in the adjoining cases, from the pottery works near the School of Art at Bombay. That work is practically Hala ware, much improved both in quality and design, with, for the most part, the artistic and judicious introduction of oriental designs from other places. It is unnecessary to do more than state that the specimens are chiefly plates and domestic vessels.

CASE NO. 280.

(PATAN POTTERY.)

Case No. 280 is filled with specimens of Patan ware. Anhilwarra Patan, in the Baroda State, was in ancient times the capital of the Balhara Raes, who were paramount lords of Western India at the beginning of our era.

There was trade between this country and the West, which seems to be clearly proved by the Roman and Greek shapes and even likeness of materials of the vessels, as for example, Red pottery, which is similar to the old Samian ware.

No. 8627. All the classic forms are, however, better shown in Case No. 284. The modern ware is black or cream coloured clay, much of which is enriched with false gilding that turns to a sort of " art " green colour after a short time. Perhaps however the most interesting are the thickly glazed grotesque figures and common vessels of various colours. The glaze is very rich and of varied colour, and, if taken in hand by a well-informed expert, might form the basis of a very superior art manufacture. Some of the figures of animals, birds, etc., both glazed and unglazed, are very amusing.

CASE NO. 281.

The large case contains some fine specimens of Bombay ware, of which the following are perhaps the best :—

No. 8697. A globular vase on a stand (total height nearly 3 feet). On a cream coloured ground are represented flowers and birds taken from the Ajunta frescoes.

No. 8698. A brown obovoid vase with a cover, on a stand, and adorned with elephant's heads in relief at the top, and on the stand. Decoration taken from the Ajunta frescoes. Height 3 feet 8½ inches.

No. 8699. A large vase with light blue ground and dark blue floral ornament. Height 2 feet 10 inches.

No. 8706. Globular vase with rich colouring in brown and green. Ajunta ornament.

No. 8707. A large globular vase. Yellow flowers on a dark brown ground. Made at Hala. Height 3 feet.

Ewers, jugs, vases, and plates from Bombay and Hala. Some of the plates are large and interesting, for example:

No. 8716. On which is depicted Indra fighting with Ravana, King of Ceylon, with a border of white geese (from Ajunta).

No. 8719. Krishna dancing with the Gopis.

No. 8720. Sind-shaped salver with arabesque (Mohamedan) decoration.

BOMBAY AND SIND POTTERY CASE NO. 283.

The contents of this case are chiefly a large and very varied and complete selection of the smaller Bombay ware. The most interesting examples are:—

No. 8723. A large jar with birds, animals, and flowers in black and white on a rich brown ground.

No. 8725. An ewer or *rubai* from Sind.

No. 8729. A Basora-shaped vase.

No. 8731. A Sind rose-water bottle.

Nos. 8732 and 8733. Plain turquoise blue Japanese shaped vases. These are not very happy illustrations, as the shapes are unsuited to the ware, and mislead the student.

No. 8737. A *hookah* bowl.

No. 8746.
No. 8761. } Sind coffee-pots.

Nos. 8768 and 8782. *Surahi*, water-bottle or *kuja*. Kashmir shapes.

Nos. 8754 and 8755. Ahmedabad-shaped jugs.

No. 8780. Benares-shaped vase.

No. 8781. A plate 15¼" diameter with a splendid bouquet of flowers in the centre.

No. 8750. Lastly, there is a large vase and cover, of pottery of a red colour ornamented with grotesque figures of animals and scrolls of leaves and flowers. It comes from Kandi in Ceylon.

RECESS CASE NO. 284.

(PATAN AND CEYLON POTTERY.)

This recess case is filled with Patan and Ceylon pottery. A description of the former has already been given (see page 80). Reference is however especially made to the classical forms, as, for example—

No. 8789. A vase in the shape of the Greek Œnochœ.

No. 8790. A Roman-shaped vessel with two perforated projections as handles to which cords can be attached.

Nos. 8792 to 8826. These are specimens of tiles and grotesque figures of men and animals from Kandi in Ceylon.

No. 8792. An oblong tile painted with grotesque figures of animals, and with scrolls in yellow, black, and red on a red ground.

No. 8794. A circular plaque, ornamented with elephants.

No. 8795. The same with geese, whose necks are intertwined.

No. 8800. An oblong tile with human figures having each two heads like birds.

Nos. 8803 to 8826. Grotesque figures of birds, reptiles, and beasts moulded in clay.

RECESS CASE NO. 289.

This recess case contains pottery from the School of Art in Madras. It was manufactured some years ago when it was thought right to introduce European forms and to decorate them with Hindu (often mythological) ornament, as, for example—

No. 8847. An English sugar bowl with discs round the bowl, showing South Indian gods, in relief.

No. 8849. A water jar with similar embellishments.

No. 8850. A Spanish-shaped vase with incised ornament.

No. 8866. A Spanish vase. The work is uninteresting, but, as regards technique, well finished.

PILLAR FRAMES NO. 292.

These are not filled yet, but a few interesting objects are exhibited in them.

Nos. 8877 to 8880. They are specimens of the well-known Agra marble plates and plaques inlaid in imitation of the beautiful panels and tombs in the Taj Mahal at Agra. The visitor should study the series of illustrations of the original Taj work in the centre room in the revolving frames (No. 187).

Sir G. Birdwood also published a very fine and complete series on the same subject, most of which was unfortunately destroyed by a fire at the publisher's. The art was no doubt introduced from Europe, and is similar to the Florentine mosaic. The famous panels which were made by Antoine de Bordeaux, one of which represents Orpheus in search of Eurydice, are in the South Kensington Museum, but were taken from the fort in Delhi.

Surgeon-General J. Murray, formerly many years a resident of Agra, did much to keep up an interest in, and revive, the art by applying it to small objects which travellers could take away with them, such as plates, boxes, and paper-weights, and even chess and backgammon tables. The marble is pure white, and the best comes from Jhiri on the Jeypore-Ulwar border, or from Makrana in Marwar, near the Sambhur salt lake.

The principal stones which are used for inlaying it are lapis lazuli, heliotrope, jaspers of different kinds, carnelian, variegated marbles, nummulitic limestone from Jeysulmere, agates and Cambay stones generally, and mother-o'-pearl, a modern and inartistic introduction. Birds are sometimes copied, as for example the Cockatoo (No. 8877); but floral decoration and arabesque border patterns are most characteristic of the work.

No. 8879 shows a bouquet of flowers copied from the screen round the tombs of Shah Jehan and his wife in the Taj Mahal at Agra.

No. 8880 has a very well executed flower in the centre. The pomegranate and Indian chrysanthemum are favourite flowers. This style of ornament might be well used in church ornaments for altars, as, for example, as has been done in the Church of the Agra Cantonment. From Agra also come two delicately carved models in alabaster of tracery windows (Nos. 8881 and 8882).

CASE NO. 293.

The Central Case (No. 293) contains specimens of English porcelain and pottery.

Nos. 8907, 8908 and 8909. Three specimens of Worcestershire ware, *viz.* :—

A vase with ivory ground having delicately painted flowers in gold and colour.

Another vase with basket-shaped handle and ornament in gold and relief.

A vessel with a double bowl. The outer layer is of delicate tracery, and has three frames in it, through which are seen minutely painted landscapes in gold and sepia, which are painted on the inner bowl.

Nos. 8910 to Doulton Ware. Most of it is the work of the animal painter, Miss Barlow. The glaze is obtained by throwing salt into the furnace at the proper time. The outlines of cattle which are incised are very clever. Examples of the works of the sisters of Miss Barlow and of Miss Groome are also shown. There are four little quaint figures (Nos. 8929, 8930, 8937 and 8938) by Tinworth, the sculptor, who has attained eminence for his work in terra-cotta, and chiefly for his talented scripture illustrations in the Guard's Chapel in London and elsewhere.

CASE NO. 294.

On one of the shelves in this case are a number of red terra-cotta figures from Lucknow, which are very good representations of different classes of people, and of their occupations, as for example, No. 8941, a *chaprasi* or office messenger ; No. 8943, a *khansama* or head table servant ; No. 8947, a lady's maid or *aya ;* No. 8952, a barber or *nai* : No. 8955, a washerman or *dhobi ;* No. 9017, a shoemaker at work ; No. 9018, a snake-charmer.

Nos. 8962 to 9010 are 48 small pith figures representing the castes, professions, and occupations of the people of South India. They were made at Kondapulli in the Madras Presidency.

Nos. 9011 to 9016. These are large clay dressed figures from Trichinopoly.

Nos. 9021 to 9051. A collection of Turkish red pottery, ornamented with false silver and gold designs.

There are thirty-one pieces forming coffee and tea sets. Some of the cups are placed in filigree holders of white metal.

Nos. 9054 to 9059. Black Turkish pottery.

Nos. 9060 to 9128. A miscellaneous collection of black and red Turkish pottery, including ash trays, pipe bowls, and mouthpieces and ewers.

All the above were bought in Stamboul, the Turkish quarter of Constantinople, or the true Byzantium, the ancient capital of the Eastern Empire.

Nos. 9052 to 9030. Two pieces of lacquered and painted pottery from Hoshiarpur in the Punjab, whence comes so much similar ware in wood.

Nos. 9129 to 9131. Three puzzle tea-pots which are filled from the bottom. They are of enamelled metal, and were bought in the Peshawar bazár, but are made in Turkestan.

WALL FRAMES.

NO. 300—NOS. 9223 TO 9226. NO. 303—NOS. 9229 TO 9232.

Four tiles are shown to illustrate different designs for wall decoration in Jeypore. A full description of this art has been published by Colonel Jacob, C.I.E., Superintending Engineer of Jeypore, and an abstract of it was given in the first chapter of this book when describing the mode of preparing and painting the pictures on the outer walls of the Museum rooms.

Nos. 9227 and 9233. Nos. 31 and 304. Two large Persian bricks with glazed surfaces. The subjects represented on them are royal princes riding or at sport. Modern work.

RECESS CASE NO. 305.

This case contains glazed blue and white pottery made in the School of Art at Jeypore, and does not need further description.

No. 9258 is a tray ornamented with flowers of different colours, but is not so successful as the characteristic ware. The tiles might be used with success in decorating articles of furniture.

The whole case is filled with Jeypore pottery, of which the following is a brief description :—

It was not until the opening of the School of Art in 1866 that pottery of any value was made in Jeypore, but since that date a large quantity has been produced; practically it is the same as that for which Delhi has been long noted. The yellow clay and felspar, which are the principal ingredients in its manufacture, are, however, obtained in the State; and the cobalt and copper, with which it is coloured, are also found near Bhagore on the property of the Raja of Khetri, a feudatory of Jeypore. The vessels are formed in moulds, and, after union of the separate parts, are coated with powdered white felspar, mixed with starch, and then painted. The blue colour, which is most characteristic of the work, is obtained from an oxide of cobalt (a specimen of this ore, which is known under the name of Syepoorite or Jeypoorite, is exhibited), and the green from an oxide of copper, which is associated with it in the mines. The ware is then dipped in a transparent glaze of glass, and when dry goes to the kiln. Only one baking is required.

The variety of the designs is immense ; in fact, the great difficulty seems to be to reproduce any particular pattern. Most of the vases which are exhibited have been decorated with arabesque patterns. Of late the potters have preferred to cover their vessels with mythological and other figures.

Clay pottery is also made. As every article is hand-painted and the designs are so rarely repeated, the prices are necessarily somewhat higher than those charged by

European potters ; but the purchaser has the pleasure of knowing, when he becomes the possessor of a Jeypore vase, as is the case with so many other articles of Indian manufacture, that he owns something that has required an individual effort of mind to produce—something, in short, which is not a mere mechanical repetition of the design of another person. Particular attention is drawn to a number of vases marked "Amber-shaped," which were reproduced from paintings on the palace walls at Amber, the old capital of Jeypore. The original designs were drawn about 200 years ago. Only four sets were made up to 1890, and at least three of these could be traced. One of the fourth, of about two dozen vessels, the writer of this handbook found in a shop at Constantinople, whither it had come, it was said, by the overland route from Persia. It was for sale as a piece of Persian ware. This is an illustration of the difficulty of tracing the origin of an oriental art.

Case No. 306.

This case is filled (with only three small exceptions) with Jeypore pottery of all shapes and sizes—preserve jars, bottles, vases of all kinds, pilgrim flasks, pots of many forms, jars, some of which are very large, buckets, ewers, *hookah* bowls, cups and plates. The collection shows the uses to which the ware can be adapted.

Nos. 9352 to 9354. These are three specimens of lacquered and painted vessels from Indurgarh on the Chambul river, a small State which has tributary relations with both Jeypore and Bundi. They are curiosities of local manufacture with no artistic merit,

Some of the Jeypore ware (Nos. 9293, 9295 and 9297) recently introduced has a delicate grass-green ground with white and red floral ornament which is admired.

CHAPTER VIII.

STONE ROOM.

Stone carving is quite a speciality of Jeypore and the surrounding districts. Stone is the most abundant building material, but except in the east, where red sandstone is available, as at Hindown, is not easily worked. Hence the houses are chiefly constructed of rubble masonry, and not, as in Jodhpore and the other western States, of elaborately carved work, for which purpose the red and blue is most suitable. Nevertheless, in the temples and palaces, good sculptured slabs and ornaments are commonly found, in the royal marble, of which several varieties are to be had in Jeypore or in the neighbouring States near the borders. The purest marble is obtained from Makrana on the borders of Marwar, west of the Sambhur Lake, but is largely utilized in Jeypore in the manufacture of images, which are sent to all parts of India, and of which a selection is exhibited. They are plain, coloured, or gilt. At Dausa, east of the capital, large numbers of idols are made, for export towards Gujerat, from a veined whitish-blue marble from Rialo, in the hills near Ulwar. A whole division of the city of Jeypore is devoted to the Silawats or stone-cutters, who, besides their ordinary work, now find employment under the Superintending Engineer, under whose guidance they have, during the past few years, turned out carvings which are much more highly finished than formerly. Figures are also carved in black and red marble, and decorative carving is executed in a cream-coloured stone which has been much admired in Europe. The quarries are situated at Bassi in the Jeypore State. The nummulitic limestones of Jeysulmere are also cut at Jeypore into slabs for pavements, and a soft chlorite from Dungarpore is worked into small images and toys. On these soft stones, as well as on steatite, the boys learn to carve. The Case No. 308 contains a number of examples of small carved articles; but the whole of the decorative marble work in the building serves to illustrate the subject in a far more complete and handsome manner.

Nos. 9368 to 9453, 9397, 9410 and 9430. A set of small black marble animals cut at Jeypore out of black marble from Baislana. These should be contrasted with four white alabaster elephants from Burma close to them (Nos. 9372 to 9375), and similar white marble figures from Makrana (Nos. 9380, 9422, 9468) and from Jhiri on the Ulwar border (Nos. 9400, 9477, 9479 and 9480).

The black or grey chlorite of Dungarpur is easily cut into small figures, and the colour is darkened by soaking the stone in oil. It is cut into figures of animals, such as elephants (Nos. 9382, 9401, 9409, 9412, 9413), buffaloes (No. 9396), leopards (No. 9398), tigers (No. 9402) and gods of all kinds.

The case also contains rather a large and good collection of figures which were carved in Western China from amygdaloid or soft variegated sandstone. The colours of the material are very skilfully employed to add to the effect of the carving. The subjects are usually grotesque and quaint, and are very characteristic of the fertility, in these directions, of the imagination of the Chinese artist.

The specimens shown here were bought in Mandalay, and came thither by way of Bhamo (Nos. 9383 to 9393, 9395, 9414 to 9421).

The best is a group of the ten great sages of China.

On one of the shelves are several models, *e.g.*, No. 9404, the great mosque and tomb of Sheikh Selim Chisti at Fatehpur Sikri, near Agra, in painted soapstone. The material is found at Mori and other places in Jeypore. The carving is executed at Agra. No. 9405 is a model of the Taj Mahal, and No. 9406 of the tomb of Itimad Dowla. Both are in white marble of Makrana, and were made at Agra.

Several plain white marble plates (Nos. 9408, 9409, 9433 to 9435) are shown, and others with inlay of precious stones from Agra (Nos. 9460 and 9465), also boxes of the same (Nos. 9436, 9438, 9442 and 9465), which obtained the prize at the Jeypore Exhibition. There is also a tray with scalloped edges and with inlaid work along the border.

Close by are some elaborately carved soapstone boxes (No. 9436) and salvers (Nos. 9460, 9461) from Agra, some of nummulitic limestone from Jeysulmere (No. 9427), a mortar from Trichinopoly (No. 9428), a paper-weight and a ruler (No. 9429). Flat boxes (No. 9442 and 9454) in carved sandstone from Kerauli stand near them.

Eleven small toys, made from a kind of meerschaum or metamorphosed clay, also come from Kerauli (Nos. 9443 to 9453).

There is also a marble cross, which was made in Jeypore (No. 9466), and an ambitious piece of sculpture in white stone, representing a cow and calf leaning against a pilaster, from Porebunder in the Bombay Presidency.

Two large Hindu idols (No. 9477) of Krishna and (No. 9478) of Maha Kali, or "All Devouring Time," stand at the end of the case.

CASE NO. 309.

(MYTHOLOGY.)

The following extracts from my "Handbook of the Jeypore Courts at the London Indo-Colonial Exhibition" sufficiently describe the contents of this case and the reasons for their inclusion in the collections.

Mythology is the key to Hindu Art, or at all events to the motive which is at the bottom of all decorative work that is done by the Hindu.

Jeypore supplies nearly all Brahmanical India with its stone images, and stone is the most orthodox material for use in temples. For these two reasons a small typical collection is shown, in which most of the common mythological forms are represented. The images have been all made on the same scale—a small one, in order that they may be the more easily studied, and great care has been taken in carving and painting the symbols by which they are distinguished. These are usually, though not always, contained in the hands, which are numerous, when it is proposed to represent omnipotence. In some cases a difference in colour is of prime importance. Moreover, most of the gods have a special vehicle, or *vahan*, which is also adored in the hope that his vicarious influence may benefit the worshipper.

It is hardly necessary to observe that there are numerous sects of Brahmanical Hindus, besides several great schismatic faiths, the most prominent of which are the Jain and Sikh.

Of orthodox Hindus (the word is used here only in a religious sense) there are two great divisions—the followers of Vishnu, and those of Shiva or Mahadeo—for practically Brahma is not worshipped in this age, and has only one important temple in all India, *viz.*, that at Pushkar, near Ajmere.

Many branches of each sect exist who revere the deity in some particular incarnation, and, although a Vaishnava or follower of Vishnu, for example, goes to temples of that deity most frequently, he does not altogether neglect Shiva. The Hindu is very catholic in his ideas, and is ready to adore any new manifestation of accredited powers. In this way a number of demi-gods are revered.

THE JAINS.

A large number of the most wealthy merchants and bankers in Rajputana follow the Jain faith. It is everywhere spoken of as a most ancient religion, "*bahot purana mat*," and recent writers have asserted that it was a prominent faith at the beginning of our era and was parallel with, if not the parent of, Buddhism.

By Brahmanical Hindus the Jains are looked upon as Atheists (*Nastic*), that is those who believe in a future state, which is only attained by the result of their own deeds (*karm*). They thus deny the power of the Almighty to influence their future.

Their duties are—(1) Mercy to all animated beings, (2) alms-giving, (3) venerating the sages when living, and worshipping their images when deceased, (4) confession of faults, and (5) religious fasting. They should avoid the sins of (1) killing, (2) lying, (3) stealing, (4) adultery, and (5) worldly-mindedness. There are two great divisions of their body—the Svetambaras, or those who worship images which are clothed and adorned with jewels; and the Digambaras, or those whose images are nude. There are, however, it is said, 84 points of distinction, one being that the latter division holds that women must undergo another birth (for they all believe in the transmigration of souls,—in other words become men before they can attain *moksh*, that is, salvation or beatitude). They all revere 24 deified saints, lords, *tirthankaras*, or *jinas*. These are all shown on two lacquered panels (Pillar Frames No. 272 : Nos. 8538 and 8539) in the Pottery Room ; and separately as stone images.

The following is a list, in order, of the *tirthankaras*, with their symbols, which are placed on the pedestals and are the means of distinguishing them. The prevailing colour is yellow or golden, but there are exceptions to this rule :—

	Names.	*Symbols.*
1.	Rishabha	A bull.
2.	Ajita	An elephant.
3.	Sambhava	A horse.
4.	Abhinandana	An ape.
5.	Sumati	A curlew.
6.	Padmaprabha	A lotus.

	Names.	*Symbols.*
7.	Suparswa	A swastica or 卐 shaped sign.
8.	Chandraprabha	The moon.
9.	Pushpadanta	An alligator.
10.	Sitala	Shrivatsa or  shaped curl.
11.	Sreyan	A rhinoceros.
12.	Vasupujya	A buffalo.
13.	Vimala	A boar.
14.	Ananta	A falcon.
15.	Dharma	A thunderbolt.
16.	Santi	An antelope.
17.	Kunthie	A goat.
18.	Ara	A nandyavarta (a peculiar sign formed of lines).
19.	Malli	A jar.
20.	Mansuvrata	A tortoise.
21.	Nimi	A blue water lily.
22.	Nemi	A conch shell.
23.	Parswanath	A hooded snake.
24.	Mahavira	A lion.

Nos. 6 and 12 have a red complexion ; 8 and 9 are fair ; 19 and 23 are blue or green ; 20 and 22 are black ; the rest are yellow or golden. The Jains also believe that there are many compartments in heaven as well as in hell. The former are usually represented as somewhat monotonous in character, while in the latter no complaint can be made of want of variety, for each inhabitant is being tormented by demons in a fashion appropriate to the sins he has committed in the world. Of course, cruelty to animals is very cruelly punished ; but the lowest depth is reached by women who have told falsehoods to their husbands.

The Jains have always been wealthy, and they have ever devoted their gains to the honour of their religion. The well-known temples at Mount Abu were built by Jains, and a magnificent fane at Sanganir, seven miles south of Jeypore, about 300 years old, attests the splendour of their gifts, and the marvellous skill of the workmen and artists, who carried out their ideas.

There is hardly anything in India more richly and elaborately decorated than the grand Jain altar at Sanganir. Most of the wealthy bankers who patronize the wood-carvers in Shekhawati are Jains. Outside rupees and the arithmetical calculation connected with their accumulation, they seem to have no idea of figures ; for their deified saints are said to have lived for many ages and their geographical measurements are illimitable. Their idea of the world is not unlike that of the Hindus, as a map of the Jain universe sufficiently shows. Seas of milk and curd surround several worlds of different kinds, and within is the home of the blessed—a sort of Garden of Eden watered by four great streams which flow out from the abode of the celestials.

The following is a list of the principal figures :—

LIST OF PRINCIPAL EXHIBITS.

No. 9482. Vishnu reposing on Anant Nag, the Serpent of Infinity (Shesha Shayya Narayana).

No. 9484. Brahma : the Creator, First Person in the Hindu Trinity.

No. 9485. Sarasvati : wife of the above ; Goddess of Speech and Learning.

Nos. 9486 to 9489. Sanaka, Sanandana, Sanatana, Sanat Kumar : the four ever-pure mind-born sons of Brahma or Vishnu.

No. 9490. Manu or Shwayambhuva : the first of the 14 Manus or great progenitors of mankind.

No. 9491. Vishnu : the Preserver, Second Person in the Hindu Trinity.

Incarnations of Vishnu.

No. 9492. Matsya, or Fish Incarnation.

No. 9493. Kachh, the Tortoise.

No. 9494. Varaha, the Boar.

No. 9495. Narasinha, the Man-Lion.

No. 9496. Vamana, the Dwarf.

No. 9497. Parashurama, Rama with the axe who slew the Kshatriyas or warrior caste.

No. 9498. Ramachandra, Rama, King of Ayudhya or Oudh.

No. 9499. Krishna, the Apollo of India.

No. 9500. Budh.

No. 9501. Kalki, the Incarnation which is yet to come.

The above ten form the greater incarnations.

No. 9502. Vyasa : author of the Puranas and arranger of the Vedas or Scriptures.

No. 9503. Raja Prithi : the first anointed King of the Earth.

No. 9504. Hari : Vishnu, incarnate to release an elephant who called on his name.

No. 9505. Hansa : the Goose or Crane who taught the Vedas to Brahma.

No. 9506. Yajna : or sacrifice personified.

No. 9507. Rishaba : king of Oudh and founder of the Jain religion.

No. 9509. Hayagriva : the horse-necked, who appeared to recover the Vedas.

No. 9510. Dhruva : the Pole Star, a worshipper of Vishnu, who became incarnate in him. He was elevated to the Pole Star.

No. 9511. Dhanwantari : physician of the gods.

No. 9512. Badrinath : Vishnu as Lord of Badrinath in the Himalayas.

No. 9513 Kapila : the Sage who destroyed the 10,000 sons of Sagara.

The above are the remaining incarnations of Vishnu.

No. 9514. Lakshmi or Shri : wife of Vishnu, and Goddess of Fortune.

No. 9515. Ganga : the Ganges river personified.

No. 9516. Krishna holding up Mount Goverdhan to protect the Cowherds against the wrath of Indra.

9545 SHIVA.

9484 BRAHMA.

9491 VISHNU.

9581 KUVERA, GOD OF WEALTH.

9521 SITA, WIFE OF RAMA.

9576 VARUNA, GOD OF THE WATERS.

XIV. STONE IMAGES.

No. 9517. Balarama: elder brother of Krishna. An incarnation of the serpent Shesha.

No. 9518. Nagnathatahua-Krishna, or Kali Mantan: Krishna as destroyer of the Serpent King, Kali, who lived in the Jumna river.

No. 9519. Chaturbhuja: the four-armed Vishnu.

No. 9520. Vishnu.

No. 9521. Sita: wife of Rama Chandra.

No. 9522. Rukmini: another wife of Krishna.

No. 9523. Hanuman: a demi-god, son of the wind and of a monkey. The great general of Rama.

No. 9524. Narada: the Sage; a friend of Krishna.

No. 9525. Garuda: the King of the Vultures, the vehicle of Vishnu.

No. 9526. Yamuna: the river Jamna personified.

No. 9527. Ananta: the King of Serpents.

No. 9528. Gokulesh: Lord of Gokul. The image is now at Kamha and was formerly at Jeypore.

No. 9529. Madan Mohan: Lord of Desire; also at Kamha, formerly at Jeypore.

No. 9530. Mathuresh: Lord of Mathura, at Kotah.

No. 9531. Vithal-nath: Pandurang: at Kotah.

No. 9532. Dwàrkanath: Lord of Dwarka. Temple at Kankaraoli in Meywar.

No. 9533. Srinath, at Nathdwara in Meywar. This is the greatest of the seven forms of Krishna (Nos. 9528 to 9534; Kader Nath, at Surat, has been omitted). If worshippers look upon them all, they can form some idea of the perfect Krishna.

No. 9534. Nava-nand Priya: the infant Krishna at Nathdwara.

No 9535. Balmukand: the infant Krishna, god of the Vallabhacharyas.

No. 9536. Shesha: the Serpent King; Lord of the lower world, who supports Krishna while sleeping on the ocean during the intervals of creation.

No. 9537. Vishwakarma: Architect of the gods.

No. 9538. Barbhaghwan: Vishnu floating on a leaf of the Indian fig on the waters before the creation.

No. 9543. Jagannathji: Vishnu as worshipped at Puri in Orissa.

No. 9544. Vishnu Vituba: Vishnu as worshipped by the Mahrattas.

We now come to Shiva and his different forms, &c.

No. 9545. Shiva or Mahadeva: Third Person of the Hindu Trinity; the Destroyer.

No. 9546. Parvati: wife or *shakti*, the female essence of Shiva.

No. 9547. Ganesha or Ganapati: the elephant-headed god of Wisdom; son of Shiva.

No. 9548. Kartikeya: god of War; son of Shiva.

No. 9549. Annapurna Devi: goddess of Food or Plenty.

There are many forms of Devi, or Uma, or Parvati, or Durga, &c.

No. 9550. Sinha Vahini Devi: she whose vehicle is the lion.

No. 9551. Mahakali: she who destroys all beings at the end of an age, or Kalpa—"All-devouring Time."

No. 9552. Mahisha Mardini Devi: as the slayer of the buffalo demon.

No. 9553. Shila Devi : the stone goddess, as worshipped at Amber.

No. 9554. Bhairava : attendant of Mahadeva.

No. 9555. The bull, Nandi : the vehicle of Shiva.

No. 9556. Triveni : the conjunction of the three rivers Ganges, Jumna, and the heavenly Sarasvati at Pryag or Allahabad. (The Ganges springs from the hair of Shiva.)

No. 9557. Panchmukhi Shiva : a *ling* or symbol of Shiva with his five heads.

No. 9559. The Ling.

No. 9560. Vira Bhadra : an attendant on Shiva.

No. 9561. Ardhanari Shiva : Shiva and Parvati in combination.

The planets follow.

No. 9562. Surya, or the Sun : Regent of the S. W. quarter.

No. 9563. Chandra, Soma, or the Moon : Regent of the N.E. quarter.

No. 9564. Mangala or Mars.

No. 9565. Budha : the planet Mercury.

No. 9566. Vrihaspati : the planet Jupiter, preceptor of the gods.

No. 9567. Shukra : the planet Venus—a male.

No. 9568. Shani : the planet Saturn.

No. 9569. Rahu : the ascending node—the head of the dragon who devours the Sun and Moon at eclipses.

No. 9570. Ketu : the descending node, or lower part of Rahu.

No. 9571. Kama : god of love—the Hindu Cupid, husband of Rati or Venus.

No. 9572. Indra : Regent of the Eastern quarter—king of Heaven, or Swarga, the first of the seven heavens.

No. 9574. Agni : god of Fire—Regent of the South-East quarter.

No. 9575. Yama : Regent of the South—god of the Dead.

No. 9576. Varuna : Regent of the West—god of the Waters.

No. 9577. Vayu : as father of Hunuman.

No. 9578. Vayu : Regent of the North-West—god of the Wind.

No. 9579. Yoni, or seat for the Ling (Black stone).

No. 9580. Kuvera : god of Wealth—Regent of the North.

No. 9581. Kuvera : riding on a man—god of Wealth.

No. 9582. Mrityu : god of Death.

No. 9583. Bhumiya : the lord of the Soil—generally a man of blood, who dies an unnatural death, and becomes a snake, which haunts the land near the place of his death, and is propitiated by the inhabitants in the hope that he will not injure them.

No. 9587.—Dattatreya : a sage in whom a portion of the Trinity became incarnate.

Next to the above are the 24 Jain Tirthankaras or deified lords, or Jinas, who are revered by that sect. They are described at page 89. At the bottom of the case are a number of wooden images from Trichinopoly, such as are used in the Madras Presidency (Nos. 9628 to 9641). In frame No. 310 is a coloured enlargement of a plate showing the chief sectarian forehead marks as worn by the different sects of Hindus. The names are given wherever possible.

FRAME NO. 311.

The *mala* or rosary of the worshipper of Shiva is most frequently made of the seeds of the *rudraksha* (the eye of Shiva) [*Eleocarpus ganitrus*] (Nos. 9666-9648, 9649, 9650, 9673 and 9674); of the adorer of Vishnu, of the wood of the *tulsi* or sweet-scented basil (*Ocymum basilicum or sanctum*) (Nos. 9651 to 9656), or of lotus seeds (*Nelumbium speciosum*), which are also sacred to his wife Lakshmi, the goddess of wealth.

Nos. 9676, 9680, 9684, 9685, 9686 and 9687. Beads of sandal wood (*Santalum album*) are also made into rosaries (*tasbih*) at Ajmere, and sold in large numbers to the Mussalman pilgrims to the sacred shrines of the Khwaja Saheb and of another saint. These are used to mark the number of times the names of God are recited, or a customary religious duty, *wazifa*, is performed. The Shivaite recites his special *mantra* or secret charm, or invocation "Om Namah Shivaya," I bow to Shiva. Sometimes he repeats the *gayatri* or text in honour of the Sun as Brahmans of other sects do. The worshippers of Vishnu generally use the *gayatri*, and of Kali the Kali *mantra*, or invocation of that goddess, which is termed Kali *vija mantra*.

At Ajmere also small wooden toothed combs are made (see Nos. 9677, 7879 and 9679). Nos. 9655 and 9672 are necklaces of coral or *munga*. These are worn on the throats of infants to protect them from fear and sudden starts and to check crying. A rosary of gold or gems is a hundred times as auspicious as any other. The rosary should be composed of pearls, coral, *rudraksha* or crystal, or the names of the god should be counted on certain finger joints. The sapphire, pearl, ruby, cat's-eye, and diamond go to make up the Vaijayanti rosary which was used by Krishna.—(Tagore.)*

Frames Nos. 314 and 316 contain specimens of silks enriched with Indian designs, which were presented by Mr. Wardle of Leck, the President of the Silk Association of Great Britain.

In No. 315 an embroidered silk Chinese banner is shown, and in Nos. 313 and 319 are embroidered bags from Benares, which are termed 'gao mukh,' because the rosary is revolved in them without being seen, so that the prayers may be said in secret.

FRAME NO. 322.

This frame is filled with numerous specimens of seals which are used by the followers of Vishnu. They are obtained at the different shrines of that deity and of his incarnations. They are generally dipped in sandal paste, and impressed on the forehead, breast or arms, and even the cheeks of the devotees, and occasionally are made red-hot and so applied. For example, at Dwarka, the place in Guzerat where Krishna died, pilgrims return with a lotus mark on the arm. It would be tedious to describe all the varieties. Some represent the *shankh* or shell, others the *chakra* or quoit, others the *gada* or mace of Krishna, and many his footmarks or *charanapaduka*. These marks are applied in the hope that the bodies of those who wear them may be carried after death direct to Vaikunth or the Heaven of Krishna.

*For a list of Buddhist rosaries see Dr. Waddell's learned work on Lamaism, or the Buddhism of Tibet.

CASE NO. 323.

(MYTHOLOGY.)

This case contains a fine collection of brass images and of articles which are used in the Hindu religious ritual. There are, however, a few Jain and Buddhist examples, which have been added for comparative purposes. It is impossible within the limits of a popular handbook to give more than a superficial view of the subject of Mythology. I will therefore be content to refer the reader to the description which is given of the stone images in Case No. 309, in the adjoining room (page 87), and proceed at once to a detailed account of the principal exhibits.

No. 9768. Buddha seated on the coils of a large cobra or *nág*, which overshadows his head. The image of Buddha is crowned with the usual flames. (Brass; Kandi, Ceylon.)

No. 9769. Image of Gautama, erect, pointing to the city on Mandalay Hill. Model of a great masonry figure, 30 or 40 feet high. (Brass.)

No. 9770. Small brass figure in an attitude of prayer, imploring the protection of the last-named figure. (Mandalay.)

No. 9771. Buddha seated, with legs crossed, and flame head ornament. (Brass; Kandi, Ceylon.)

No. 9772. Figure of Buddha, erect, engraved, with the right hand raised as a preacher of the law. (Brass; Kandi, Ceylon.)

No. 9773. Figure of a girl in a dancing attitude, standing on a pedestal. A good example of the Hindu artist's idea of grace and beauty. (Brass; Jeypore.)

No. 9774. Parasnath, the 23rd Jain Lord, with the many-headed serpent overshadowing his head, and the cobra, his sign, on the pedestal. (Brass; Jeypore.) This should be contrasted with the figures of Buddha.

No. 9775. *Sakhi* holding a lamp. The *sakhi* is the female attendant on a deity. The male attendant is called "Parshada" or "Gana." (Brass; Jeypore.)

No. 9778. Image of Dattatreya, son of Atri and Anusaya. A Brahman saint in whom a portion of Brahma, Vishnu, and Shiva, or more particularly Vishnu, was said to be incarnated.

No. 9780. Garuda, the vehicle of Vishnu. (Brass; Jeypore.)

No. 9782. Annapurna Devi, the goddess of plenty and of food. (Brass; Jeypore.)

No. 9784. Rama, with Sita or Janaki, his wife, seated on his thigh. (Brass; Jeypore).

No. 9786. Balmukand, or the infant Krishna, worshipped by the Vallabhacharyas. (Brass; Jeypore.)

No. 9799. Chaturbhuj, or the four-armed Vishnu. (Brass; Jeypore.)

No. 9800. Shiva and Parvati riding on a bull, with Ganesha on the lap of Parvati. (Brass; Jeypore.)

No. 9803. Image of Dattatreya: a sage in whom a portion of the Trinity (Trimurti) became incarnate. Behind is a bull licking his feet, and beside him are two dogs, all very natural. A very fine image. (Copper; Bombay.)

No. 9806. Shiva Panchayatana, or a group of the five household deities. All highly finished. Shiva supports his wife Parvati and his son Ganesha. In front is Nandi, his bull, and behind are two attendants, while musicians blow horns in his honour before him. (Brass ; Bombay.)

No. 9807. Brass figure of Jagannath or Krishna as worshipped at Puri in Orissa.

No. 9812. Hanuman, the deified chief of the monkeys, carrying the healing herb *sanjivani* with a part of the mountain Himalaya in one hand, and a mace in the other. (Brass ; Burhanpur.)

No. 9813. Ganesha, the god of Wisdom, invoked at the beginning of all work, sitting on a throne. The Hindu Janus. (Brass ; Burhanpur.)

No. 9814. Garuda, the Vulture King, sitting on a throne, having a cobra's hood above him, he being the enemy and devourer of all serpents, and the *vahan* or vehicle of Vishnu. (Brass.)

No. 9816. Vishnu standing on a pedestal with the many-headed Sheshnag or the snake king overshadowing him. (Copper ; Jeypore.)

No. 9820. Model of a Buddhist tope. (Brass ; Kandi, Ceylon.)

No. 9824. Brass dish supported on the back of Garuda : used to contain offerings to the idol. In this instance termed Vishnu Kanwal. (Brass ; Bombay.)

No. 9825. Brass dish supported by a goose, the vehicle or vahana of Saraswati, wife of Brahma. (Nassik.)

No. 9826. Dish supported on a horse, the vehicle of Surya or the Sun. (Brass ; Nassik.)

No. 9830. Brass peacock, vehicle of Kartikeya, the god of War (Nagpur).

No. 9833. Lamp with oil dish on the top in the form of a *yoni* (symbol of the Shakti).

Nos. 9834 to 9850. Seventeen specimens of the *chambu*, or water-vessel, which is used by pilgrims to bring to their homes the sacred water of the Ganges (*Gangajala*). A small quantity of Ganges water is poured into the mouths of the dying by Hindus, as they are thus supposed to be assured of salvation. It is also employed in temples for libation, for bathing images, and, by addition of a drop or two, to consecrate common water to religious uses.

No. 9848. *Abkhora :* water vessel, with engraved cones round the bowl.

No. 9851. Yashoda : mother of Krishna, holding her son in her arms. More realistic than such images usually are. Very similar to many European images of the Virgin Mary. (Brass ; Jeypore.)

Nos. 9853 to 9864. Series of twelve ornamented brass figures, representing the principal gods worshipped at Gaya, to which all Hindus endeavour to go to perform the *pind-dana* ceremony, by which their ancestors are released from the bondage of this world, and are rendered capable of ascending to heaven.

No. 9865. Lotus seat for the Ling, composed of a bowl with separate leaves which can be closed so as to cover the symbol when it is placed in the receptacle. The whole is borne on the back of the bull Nandi. (Brass ; Nassik.)

No. 9879. Spoon with Ganesha on the handle. (Jeypore.) A European shape, but with the handle in the same plane as the bowl, as in Indian spoons. At the top is an image of Krishna surmounted by a many-headed snake. Made in imitation of an Apostle spoon by an ignorant workman for sale to Europeans.

Nos. 9880 to 9886. Seven temple spoons with knobs at the top. (Brass; Benares.)

Nos. 9888 to 9889. Two spoons. Krishna at the top with a cow at the bottom of a twisted handle. (Brass; Poona.)

Nos. 9890 and 9891. Two spoons. Annapurna Devi, the goddess of Food, at the top of the handle. These are genuine Indian temple spoons.

No. 9894. Charm engraved with a hymn giving the names of the Sun, which are used in his worship. (Copper; Nassik.)

No. 9900. Rude figure of Nandi (bull), the vehicle of Shiva. (Brass; Jeypore.)

No. 9906. Dish for the god Ganesh or Ganapati supported on a rat with its forelegs raised holding a ball of sweetmeat. The rat is the vehicle of Ganesh. (Nassik.)

No. 9913. Incense burner, Jain type, with two oval bowls below and a circular one above. It is also used for holding sandal paste, flowers, and rice for worship or *puja*.

No. 9921. Copper vessel (*kunda*), square shaped, to contain holy fire at the time of *havana* (sacrifice), also used to bathe the gods in it. (Nassik.)

No. 9923. *Gangajali;* vessel to hold the sacred waters of the Ganges, with a spout and the head of the goddess Ganga at the top; used in temples. The priests drop the water into the hands of the worshippers at the temples. (Brass; Jeypore.)

Case No. 324.
(Sacrificial Utensils.)

This case is filled with a number of articles which are used in Hindu worship or *puja*.

Nos. 9933 and 9936. Bells with figures, on the top of the handle, of Garuda, the Vulture King; used by members of the Vaishnava sect. A bell is rung to direct attention to the fact that the ceremonial has begun, or that a certain fresh stage in it has commenced.

No. 9938. Bell with Nandi, the bull or vehicle, on the top. Used by Shivaites. See also Nos. 9936, 9943 and 9961.

No. 9935. Sakhi. A figure, which is placed in the shrines of goddesses, and represents a female attendant.

No. 9937. A small silver plated shrine or box used by Buddhists in Tibet to contain a clay image, usually of a saint.

In the collection are numerous examples of lamps which are used in all shrines. A Hindu in the morning, after bathing and reciting the *gayatri* or sacred text 108 times, worships an image which varies according to his particular sect. Thus, for example, a follower of Vishnu first bathes the image in a copper bowl termed *tarpana* or the *arghapatr* (No. 9956), and then wipes it with a cloth called *angavastra*. Sandalwood paste is then painted on the forehead. Flowers and rice are put on the image or symbol of the god, incense is burned before the image, and a lamp and food, such as sweetmeats, &c., are placed in front. Water is now poured round the tray which contains the food, in which a small leaf of the tulsi plant (*Ocymum sanctum*) has been placed, *mantras* or verses are read from the Vedas (Purusha-Sukta) at different stages. The worship concludes with the *artika* or waving a lighted lamp before the god and the ceremonial of *pushpanjali* or scattering flowers over the image. The evening worship differs somewhat from that of the morning, and in the case of Shiva or other gods, slight changes are also made.

There are numerous specimens of the *artika*, a lamp used for waving before the god, the best of which are Nos. 9939 and 9940, each with five wicks; No. 10,005, with a peacock-shaped handle; No. 10,007, with twelve bowls for wicks; No. 10,008, with five lamps. The lamps on stands are used for lighting, as for example Nos. 9998 to 9972. No. 9949 is a *katora* or cup of copper used for offering flowers; No. 9947, a *sampatni*, another vessel for the same purpose. No. 9952, a brass tray or *sthali* for the food.

Nos. 9954, 9956, 9957. These are vessels used for pouring out libations in honour of the sun.

No. 9958. *Panchpatra*, or vessel for holding the water which is taken out by a spoon for laving the image, &c.

No. 9960. A small *yoni-ling*, which represents the combined symbols of Shiva and his wife, the male and female elements in one. It has a curved stand for holding a vessel termed *abhisheka patra*, which is filled with water. There is a small hole in the bottom, so that the water may pour drop by drop on the *lingam* (Hindi *ling* or *linga*) to keep it cool.

Nos. 9963, 9964, &c. Specimens of incense-burners of different shapes—*dhupdan*.

No. 9966. Tripod (*shankh ki parghi*) to hold the shell or *shankh*, which is used in pouring water over Vishnu.

No. 9978. Brass cup for sandal paint.

No. 9994. This is a *hindola* or swing for Shiva Panchayatana, or a group of five Hindu household deities. In the centre is the *ling*, overshadowed by a cobra coiled round the *yoni*; near it are Ganesha, God of Wisdom, and Parvati as Annapurna Devi (goddess of Food), and Nandi, Shiva's vehicle. The *hindola* more properly should be reserved for Vishnu, whose image is swung in the monsoon, as the god is supposed to rest during that season, but this specimen was obtained from Nassik, where the Shivaite sect is most strongly represented.

No. 9995. A *jalahri* or seat for the *ling*, with a hood of serpents. The cobra is especially connected with the worship of Shiva.

No. 10012. *Kamandalu*; a devotee's gourd-shaped begging bowl.

No. 9983. *Gangajali*, or bottle for Ganges water.

No. 10021. A throne (*sinhasana*) for an idol. It is so called because it is generally borne by tigers or lions or the feet of those animals. This was a very ancient Assyrian custom.

No. 10034. *Imarti*: a water vessel to contain *amrit* or nectar, that is, Ganges water.

No. 10036. *Vasudeva*, or tantalus cup. This is a toy sold at Mathura to commemorate the retreat of the waters of the Ganges, when they touched the feet of the infant Krishna as he was being carried over the Jamna River by Vasudeva. The cup empties as soon as the water touches the little figure in the middle.

CHAPTER IX.

MYTHOLOGICAL ROOM.

FRAMES NOS. 326 TO 330.

Collections of coins are of the utmost value in illustrating the history of a country as well as the art of the metallurgist. The coins of India and Kabul are of especial value, not only because we are able to trace in them the art history of the country, but to discover much that it owes to outside influences, as for example to the Greeks. It would be most costly, if not impossible, to procure a perfect series of coins relating to India. Moreover, two sets would be necessary in order that the obverse and reverse of each coin might be shown, and, even if these were obtained, the public display of so much valuable and portable wealth would be attended with great risk. Fortunately, through the enterprize of the British Museum authorities, it is now possible to obtain complete electrotype collections of coins, which serve every useful purpose. A set of these will be found in five frames (Nos. 326 to 330).

They begin with the coins of the Greek kings of Kabul and India. The coins of Antiochus II, who reigned in Bactria shortly after the death of Alexander, are remarkably like those of the great conqueror himself, but some of the later ones are more artistic, as for example those of Euthydemus II, Eucratides and Plato; but all show clearly that they are the work of Greek artists or of their pupils. It is needless to refer particularly to the Indo-Scythic kings whose coins follow, but it will be clear to the most superficial observer that there is a rapid degeneration, in both execution and design, until the coins of the early Hindu kings, in Frame No. 328, become so debased as to preserve no trace of art whatever, and the heads of the kings are hardly recognisable as even human. The inscriptions also degenerate quite as rapidly. The coins of the Mohamedan rulers of India, with the exception of the zodiacal series of Jehangir, bear inscriptions only. Some of these are handsome enough, being in the Kufic and other ornamental Arabic and Persian characters, which in themselves are beautiful. It is probable that if the Musalmans had not objected to portraiture, they would have produced an artistic coinage. A short account of the history of each period will be given by way of introduction.

FRAME NO. 326.—NOS. 10004 TO 10102.

(ELECTROTYPES OF COINS.)

The coins shewn in this collection are electrotypes from originals in the British and other Museums. The whole series fairly represents the coinage of India from the death of Alexander the Great. In most cases the obverse and reverse of the coin are shewn. Many of the early kings reigned contemporaneously, and very few dates of the rule of individuals are known. Moreover, the dates of the dynasties are in some instances only conjectural.

GREEK KINGS OF KABUL AND INDIA.

After the death, in B.C. 323, of Alexander the Great, who conquered Kabul and traversed North India to the river Jhelum, Bactria or North Kabul, became an independent sovereignty under Greek Chiefs, whose rule extended at times to the mouth of the Indus. It is believed, chiefly from the evidence of coins, that there were between B.C. 520 and B.C. 120 a number of independent princes who ruled over Kabul and the Punjab, and used the Western Pali language, which was allied to Sanscrit. They worshipped Greek and Turanian deities, and in the eastern part of the country were Buddhists. They were finally overcome by an eruption of Scythian tribes from the centre of Asia.

1, Antiochus II; 2, Antiochus II; 3, Antiochus II; 4, Sophytes; 5, Diodotus; 6, Diodotus; 7, Euthydemus I; 8, Euthydemus I; 9, Demetrius; 10, Demetrius; 11, Euthydemus II; 12, Euthydemus; 13, Pantaleon; 14, Agathocles and Euthydemus; 15, Agathocles and Diodotus; 16, Agathocles and Alexander; 17, Agathocles; 18, Agathocles; 19, Antimachus; 20, Eucratides; 21, Eucratides; 22, Plato; 23, Eucratides with Heliocles and Laodice; 24, Eucratides with Heliocles and Laodice; 25, Heliocles; 26, Heliocles; 27, Antialcides; 28, Antialcides; 29, Lysias; 30, Lysias; 31, Diomedes; 32, Archebius; 33, Archebius; 34, Archebius; 35, Apollodotus I; 36, Strato; 37, Strato; 38, Agathoclea; 39, Menander; 40, Menander; 41, Menander; 42, Apollodotus II; 43, Epander; 44, Dionysius; 45, Zoilus; 46, Apollophanes; 47, Antimachus II; 48, Philoxenus; 49, Philoxenus; 50, Nicias; 51, Hippostratus; 52, Amyntas; 53, Amyntas; 54, Hermœus; 55, Hermœus and Calliope.

FRAME II—NO. 327.

(INDO-SCYTHIC KINGS OF NORTH INDIA.)

Hermœus, the last ruler of the Bactrian Kingdom of Nysa, was overthrown by Kadphises, head of an Indo-Scythian clan. The dynasty to which this prince belonged ruled from the beginning of the first century before Christ to about the end of the second century after Christ and ended with Vasudeva. Kashmir was also under this rule. Inscriptions of some of the kings have been found as far south as Mathura.

The coins from Nos. 1 to 28 are those of the Parthian Kings of Bactria. The Parthians were a tribe of Scythians whose rule extended over most of Asia about B.C. 250. They fell before the Persians. On many of these coins are distinct traces of Roman influence, indicating intercourse of some kind with Italy, probably through Parthia, which extended to Merv-ul-rud on their own borders. They were unconquered by the Romans. The religion of this kingdom was Sivaite at first, but afterwards Buddhistic. The demand for these coins has been so great as to lead to forgery of some of them being attempted.

1, Ranjabala; 2, Maues; 3, Maues; 4, Azes; 5, Azes; 6, Azes; 7, Azes; 8, Azes; 9, Azilises; 10, Azilises; 11, Azilises; 12, Azilises; 13, Vonones and Spalahores; 14, Vonones and Spalagdames; 15, Spalirises and Spalagdames; 16, Spalirises and Azes; 17, Spalarises; 18, Gondophares; 19, Gondophares; 20, Abdalgases; 21, Zeionises; 22, Sanabares; 23, Pacores; 24, Orthagnes; 25, Megas Soter; 26, Heraus; 27, Kodes; 28, Kodes; 29, Kadphises I; 30, Kadphises; 31, Kadphises II; 32, Kadphises II; 33, Kadphises II; 34, Kadphises II; 35, Kanerkes Athro; 36, Kanerkes Ardochro; 37, Kanerkes Arooaspo; 38, Kanerkes Boddo; 39, Kanerkes Mao; 40, Kanerkes Nanarao; 41, Kanerkes Orlagno; 42, Kanerkes Salene; 43, Kanerkes Helios; 44, Kanerkes Nanaia; 45, Ooerkes Araeiclero; 46, Ooerkes Herakilo; 47, Ooerkes Maaseno; 48, Ooerkes Manobago; 49, Ooerkes Ma and Miro;

50, Ooerkes Oaninda; 51, Ooerkes Okro; 52, Ooerkes Raorethro; 53, Ooerkes Sarapo; 54, Ooerkes Skanda, etc.; 55, Ooerkes Pharro; 56, Vasudeva; 57, Vasudeva; 58, Indo-Scythic Imitation; 59, Indo-Scythic Imitation; 60, Indo-Scythic Imitation; 61, Indo-Scythic Imitation.

CLASS III.—FRAME NO. 328.—NOS. 10164 to 10219.
(EARLY HINDU KINGS.)

The earliest Buddhist coins are supposed to be those of the series found at Behat in the Doab, and known as Punch coins. They are indeed the earliest specimens of Hindu currency, and are found all over India.

The Chalukya Dynasty, a branch of the Rajput race, is the oldest of which we have record in the Dekhan.

A branch of the Sassanian family ruled in Northern India and Kabul between the 3rd and 6th centuries. Their coins are frequently found. Coins have been found of dynasties of kings who reigned after the fall of the Indo-Scythic Kings or perhaps at the same time with some of them. Of these the best known are the Sah Kings of Surashtra or Guzerat, and the Gupta family, who, according to Mr. Thomas, succeeded them, and were followed by the Valabhi Kings and Indo-Sassanians.

The Guptas ruled from about A.D. 166 to A.D. 319. Their coins have been found in great numbers at Kanoj. Their capitals were at Kanoj and Patna, and their empire probably included a very large part of India, extending from Guzerat to beyond Patna.

The Sah Kings reigned from about the 1st century B.C. to the 3rd century A.D. Vira Dama and Isvara Datta ruled after A.D. 97, and Vijaya Sah A.D. 115, Visva Sinha A.D. 143, and Rudra Sinha in A.D. 173 or 213—(Newton).

The Gupta Surashtran Kings of Guzerat date about as follow:—Kumara, about A.D. 200; Skanda, 209; Toramana, 261.

The kingdom of Kanoj lasted from the 8th to the 12th century. The Rathors were of a family which ruled from about A.D. 1050 to 1193. Sahasanka reigned about A.D. 900, and Kumarpal about A.D. 1096.

The Sunga or Mitra Dynasty reigned in Rohilkand about the same time as the Guptas, from the 2nd and 1st centuries before to the 2nd century after Christ.

The Ceylon dynastic list is a long one, going back to B.C. 543. Lankesvara, an usurper, reigned about A.D. 1060; Lankesvara, another ruler, A.D. 1215.

The Kashmir mythical list is even still longer, as it goes back to B.C. 3714.

Of the coins, those of Yasa are the earliest shown; date A.D. 939 or 960, Kshema, 950 or 971; Jaya Sinha, 1127 or 1088. The era of the Samanta Deva series of coins is not very certain. Prithi Raja died in 1193. Most of these coins have the Samanta Deva device on them, and perhaps are of the period preceding or about the time of the conquest of Shahab-u-din Ghori or Mohamad Bin Sam.

1, Punched coin; 2, Punched coin; 3, Punched coin; 4, Punched coin; 5, Chalukya dynasty; 8, Kunada, brother of Amogha; 9, Indo-Sassanian; 10, Indo-Sassanian; 11, Indo-Sassanian; 12, Indo-Sassanian Kanoj; 13, Gupta Vasudeva; 14, Gupta Ghatotkacha; 15, Gupta Chundra Gupta; 16, Gupta Samudra; 17, Gupta Samudra; 18, Gupta Samudra; 19, Gupta Samudra; 20, Gupta Chundra Gupta II; 21, Gupta Kumara; 22, Gupta Skanda;

23, Gupta Mahendra; 24, Gupta; 25, Sasangka; 26, Rathor, Kumarapala; 27, Rathor, Prithvideva; 28, Sunga Agnimitra; 29, Sunga Indramitra; 30, Ceylon, Lankesvara; 31, Ceylon, Lankesvara; 32, Ceylon, Iraka; 33, Ceylon, Parakama; 34, Nepal, early; 35, Kashmir, Yasa; 36, Kashmir, Pratapa; 37, Kashmir, Vinada; 38, Kashmir, Toramana; 39, Kashmir, Koshema; 40, Kashmir, Abhimana; 41, Kashmir, Jayasinha; 42, Rajput, Kabul, Vankadeva; 43, Rajput, Syalapatideva; 44, Rajput, Samantadeva; 45, Rajput, Samantadeva; 46, Rajput, Prithvi Raja; 47, Rajput, Chahada Raja, SAURASTRAN; 48, Sah, Viradama; 49, Sah, Isvaradatta; 50, Sah, Vijaya Sah; 51, Sah, Visva Sinha; 52, Sah, Rudra Sinha; 53, Gupta Kumara; 54, Gupta Kumara; 55, Gupta Skanda; 56, Gupta Toramana.

CLASS IV.—FRAME 329—NOS. 10220 TO 10271.

(PATHAN KINGS OF DELHI.)

The last Hindu ruler of Delhi and Ajmere, Prithi Raj, Chohan, was defeated in A.D. 1193 by Shahab-u-din Ghori, who left Kutb-u-din as governor. When Shahab-u-din was assassinated, Kutb-u-din became Sultan of Delhi. He reigned from A.D. 1206 to 1210. Altamsh, his successor, who had been a slave like himself, died in 1236.

Sultana Reziah—a woman, daughter of Altamsh, ruled from 1236 to 1239. The date of accession of the sovereigns after her are as follow:—Moiz-u-din Behram 1239, Ala-u-din Masud 1241, Nasir-u-din Mahomed 1246, Gheias-u-din Balban 1266, Moiz-u-din Kaikobad 1286.

HOUSE OF KHILJI.

Jelal-u-din Firoz II. 1288, Rukn-u-din Mubarik 1295, Ala-u-din Khilji II. 1295, Kutb-u-din Mubarik 1317, Nasir-u-din 1321, who murdered his predecessor, and in turn was slain by the governor of the Punjab, who founded the

HOUSE OF TOGHLUK.

Gheias-u-din 1321, Mahomed bin Toghluk 1325, Feroz Toghluk 1351, Nasir-u-din 1385, expelled in 1389, Gheias-u-din II. 1389, Abubekr Toghluk 1389, Nasir-u-din returned in 1389, Mahomed Toghluk II. 1394, Daulat Khan Lodi 1414.

THE SEIADS.

Delhi was ruled for 36 years by the Seiads, whose dominion extended little beyond its walls. There were four of this family—Khizr Khan 1414, Mubarik 1421, Mahomed 1435, Ala-u-din 1444.

THE HOUSE OF LODI.

Behloli Lodi 1450, Secunder Lodi 1481, Ibrahim Lodi 1517. He was killed at the battle of Paniput in 1526, by Baber, the founder of the house of Timur. Baber was succeeded in 1530 by Humayun, who was expelled by Sher Shah, in 1540.

HOUSE OF SUR.

Sher Shah 1540, Selim Shah Sur 1545, Mahomed Shah Sur Adil 1553, Sekandar Sur, king of only part of the empire, 1554.

Humayun re-established himself at Delhi in 1555, and died in 1556, being succeeded by Akbar, who welded the different kingdoms of India into one empire.

Bengal revolted from Mohamed Toghluk about 1338 and remained under the separate rule of Mohamedan kings until 1573. Nos. 29 to 44 are the coins of some of these rulers.

The Kingdom of Jaunpur, or Kingdom of the East, lasted from 1394 to 1478. There were six kings, of two of whom coins are shewn (Nos. 45 and 46).

The Guzerat Kingdom was founded by Mozuffer Shah in 1396, and ended with its conquest by Akbar in 1572. No. 47 is a coin of Mahmud II. of this family.

Malwa became independent in the reign of Sultan Firoz Toghluk under Dilawar Ghori, A.D. 1401. The capital was at Mandu. Bahadur Shah II. of Guzerat conquered and annexed the country in A.D. 1531. Gheias-u-din (coin No. 50) reigned from A.D. 1482 to 1500, and Nasir-u-din (coin No. 51) from 1500 to 1512.

The Bahmani Kings of Afghan descent ruled over the Dekhan from A.D. 1347 to A.D. 1526. The coins of Firuz, 1397, and Humayun, 1457, are shewn. The capital was first at Kulbarga, and afterwards at Bidar.

Sultan Kuli Kutb Shah, a Turkoman of Hamadan in Persia, founded the Golconda dynasty, which ruled from A.D. 1512, and ended with Mahomed Kuli, who succeeded in 1580. Ibrahim reigned from 1550 to 1580.

1, Mohammad Ibn Sam; 2, Mohammad Ibn Sam; 3, Kanauj Mohammad Ibn Sam; 4, Shems-ed-deen Altemsh; 5, Shems-ed-deen Altemsh; 6, Sultana Reziah; 7, Ala-ed-deen Mesood; 8, Nasir-ed-deen Mahmood; 9, Ghiyash-ed-deen Balban; 10, Muizz-ed-deen Kaikobad; 11, Jalal-ed-deen Feroz II; 12, Rukn-ed-deen Ibraheem; 13, Ala-ed-deen Mohammad; 14, Kutb-ed-deen Mubarak; 15, Nasir-ed-deen Khusru; 16, Ghiyash-ed-deen Tughlak; 17, Mohammad Ibn Tughlak; 18, Mohammad Ibn Tughlak; 19, Mahmood Ibn Mohammad; 20, Firoz III; 21, Nasir-ed-deen Mohammad; 22, Mahmood Ibn Mohammad; 23, Mohammad Ibn Fereed; 24, Behloli Lodi; 25, Sher Shah; 26, Islam Shah; 27, Mohammad Adil.

PATHAN KINGS OF BENGAL.

28, Sekender; 29, Ghiyash-ed-deen Bahadur; 30, Shems-ed-deen Feroz; 31, Ala-ed-deen Alee; 32, Shems-ed-deen Ilyas; 33, Sekander Ibn Shems-ed-deen; 34, Ghiyash-ed-deen Azim Shah; 35, Jalal-ed-deen Mohammad Ibn Khansa; 36, Shems-ed-deen Yoosuf Ibn Barbek; 37, Sekander; 38, Ala-ed-deen Huseyn; 39, Nasir-ed-deen Ibn Huseyn; 40, Mahmood Ibn Huseyn; 41, Mohammad Gezee; 42, Bahadur Ibn Mohammad; 43, Jelal-ed-deen Ibn Mohammad; 44, Dadoo Khan Ibn Suleyman.

KINGS OF THE EAST.

45, Shems-ed-deen Ibraheem; 46, Mahmood Ibn Ibraheem Shah.

KINGS OF GUJRAT.

47, Mahmood II.

BAHAMNEES.

48, Taj-ed-deen Fenz; 49, Humayoon.

KINGS OF MALWA.

50, Ghiyash-ed-deen ; 51, Nasir-ud-deen.

KINGS OF GOLCONDA.

52, Ibraheem.

CLASS V.—FRAME NO. 330—NOS. 10272 TO 10324.

(MOGHUL EMPERORS OF DELHI.)

Baber, the 6th in descent from Tamerlane, took Delhi in 1526, and was succeeded by Humayun in 1530. Akbar, who established his dominion over most of India, reigned from 1556 to 1605. Some of his coins are square.

The dates of accession of the remaining sovereigns of this line are :—

Jehangir ...	... 1605	Farokshah ...	1713	Alamgir II ...	... 1754
Shah Jehan	... 1628	Rafi-u-Dirjat	1719	Shah Alam ...	... 1759
Aurangzeb...	... 1658	Rafi-u-Daula	1719	Akbar Shah ...	... 1806
Bahadur Shah	... 1707	Mohamad Shah	1719	Bahadur Shah	... 1837
Jahandar Shah	... 1712	Ahmad Shah ...	1748		

The last Moghul was deposed in 1857.

Amongst the coins will be found a set, which is known as the zodiacal series of Jehangir, on account of the sign of the zodiac engraved upon them.

The conquest of Nepal by the Goorkhas took place in A.D. 1768. Prior to this, for 150 years, the valley of Khatmandu was divided into the three sovereignties of Patan, Bhatgaon, and Khatmandu.

No. 43 is a Khatmandu coin of about 1715 ; No. 44 a Patan coin of about 1654 ; and No. 45 one of 1744 ; and No. 46 one of Bhatgaon of the 17th century ; No. 47 is a coin of Prithi Narayan, the first Goorkha Raja ; No. 48 one of later date.

The mythical history of Nepal dates back to B.C. 3803.

The Indrayansa Dynasty made Assam independent about A.D. 1230.

Chakradvaja reigned about 1621, and Rajesvara Sinha in 1751.

The list of MANIPUR RAJAS begins in A.D. 351. Gauri Singh ruled in 1758.

46, Mahmood Ibn Ibraheem Shah.

1, Zeheer-ed-deen Baber ; 2, Humayoon Ibn Baber ; 3, Jelal-ed-deen Akbar ; 4, Jelal-ed-deen Akbar ; 5, Jelal-ed-deen Akbar ; 6, Jelal-ed-deen Akbar ; 7 to 22, Noor-ed-deen Jehangeer, Jehangeer and Noor Jehan ; 24, Shah Jehan ; 25, Shah Jehan ; 26, Shuja-a-Shah ; 27, Murad Baksh ; 28, Aurangzeb ; 29, Azim Shah ; 30, Bahadur Shah ; 31, Jehangeer Shah ; 32, Ferokhshah ; 33, Rafi-ud-Darjat ; 34, Rafi-ud-Dawlah ; 35, Mohammad Shah ; 36, Ahmad Shah ; 37, Alumgir Sani ; 38, Shah Jehan II ; 39, Shah Alam ; 40, Mohamad Akbar II ; 41, Bahadur Shah II ; 42, Oudh.

NEPAL.

43, KHATMANDU, Chakravartendra Malla ; 44, PATAN, Vira Siddhi Nara Sinha ; 45, PATAN, Prakasa Malla ; 46, BHATGAON, Jagat Prakasa ; 47, Prithi Narayana ; 48, Siddhi Lakshmi Devi.

ASSAM.

49, Ahom; 50, Chakradvaja; 51, Rajeśvara Sinha; 52, MANIPURA, Gavra Sinha; 53, Ram Tangka.*

MAPS OF INDIA.

On the walls of this room are shown four maps, which I have prepared, from various sources, to illustrate and explain the history of India in connection with the frames of coins close by them.

On map No. 335 will be found the divisions of India, as far as they can be ascertained from the coins themselves and from the Ramayana and Mahabharata, for the period between about 1500 B.C. and 1000 A.D. Map No. 325 shows the political divisions of India in 637-639 A.D., and the route taken by Hwen Thsang, a celebrated Chinese pilgrim. The march of Alexander the Great into India is also marked out (compiled from General Cunningham's Ancient Geography of India).

Map No. 331 is devoted to the Mohamedan period, or from the expeditions of Mahmud of Ghuzni into India down to the battle of Plassey (the beginning of the eleventh century to 1757 A.D.).

The lines of invasion of Mahmud of Ghuzni, of Shahab-u-din Ghori, of Timur, of Baber, of Nadir Shah, and Ahmad Shah Durani are indicated.

On map No. 332 is represented the growth of the British power in India. The dates of acquisition of the early English settlements are given, also the routes of Sir T. Roe in 1615-1618, and of Tavernier and other early European travellers.

The additions at the time of Clive, 1750 to 1771, and again to Warren Hastings, before 1785, are shown; and, by suitable colours and marks, the boundaries of British territory in 1798, 1805, 1823 and 1887 are also indicated.

Armegon was the first British fortified station in 1628. Madras the first British possession in 1640.

---

* NOTE.—The above account is chiefly compiled from the Centenary Review of the Asiatic Society of Bengal. The spelling follows that in the frames of the British Museum.

CHAPTER X.

CASE NO. 336—ANTIQUITIES.

EGYPTIAN SECTION.

Case No. 336 contains a completely representative collection of Egyptian Antiquities which was made especially for the Jeypore Museum by H. E. Brugsch Bey, Curator of the Museum at Cairo. As all the articles are genuine, and have been selected by one of the principal authorities on the subject, the student will find here all that is really necessary to obtain a good insight into the subject of Egyptology, and to make his future studies full of interest. Should he wish for more, he can examine with advantage the series of photographs of the most valuable objects in the Cairo Museum, which have already been described, the mummy in Case No. 337, and a *fac-simile* of the Papyrus of Ani, on the wall of the passage between the East and Central Rooms on the upper floor of the Museum. The following is a summary of the contents of Case No. 336 :—

Nos. 10332 to 10337. Funeral or *ushabtu* figures (figurines). These were deposited in the tombs either in wooden boxes or were laid along the floor. They were supposed to do for the deceased whatever work was decreed for him in the under-world, and bear upon them an inscription from the Book of the Dead. The Egyptians, as is well known, believed in a resurrection from the dead of the body, the intelligence, and the soul, and held it of great importance that the body of the deceased should be preserved in readiness for the reunion of the two latter with it : hence the practice of embalming, so that the dead body or mummy might be preserved indefinitely. Most of the figures are made of a semi-vitrified ware, which, according to Sir G. Birdwood, is similar to that now made in Jeypore and Delhi into ornamental vessels of all kinds. They vary in colour from light green to very dark blue, the latter (Nos. 10344 and 10345) being specially characteristic of those which were found in 1881 at Deir-el-Bahari with the mummies of Rameses the Great and other Pharoahs. No. 10337, bearing the name of "Psametic Senb of the 26th Dynasty" (B.C. 665 to 527), is particularly handsome. Another (No. 10387) of Psametichus, who was conquered by Cambyses, king of Persia, is also fine. It is of a light grey stone. Some of the figures are made of clay.

Next in importance to the figures are numerous small amulets (Nos. 10583 to 10619 and 10624 to 10633), which were swathed in the bandages of the mummy, or placed in the chest, and were supposed to help the dead in his many trials with wild beasts and demons, and in all the labours he had to undergo before soul, intelligence, and mummy were reunited. Amongst these were the tat (Nos. 10617, 10618, 10619), the emblem of stability; Ta the buckle of a girdle, which places the dead under the protection of Isis ; the column, signifying verdure or freshness, Nos. 10625, 10626, 10627 ; the symbolic eye representing health and well-being, Nos. 10649 to 10677 (a rare specimen). There are also the signs of life (No. 10630), and of love, the heart (Nos. 10604 to 10606), right angle (No. 10600) triangle (Nos. 10602 and 10603), pillow (No. 10587), pyramid (Nos. 10597 to 10599). They are made of many substances, as of porcelain (No. 10592); glass, lapis lazuli (Nos. 10612, 10614 and 10617); hæmatite (Nos. 10600, 10601, 10602 and 10605); and carnelian (Nos. 10606, 10607 and 10610).

In the collection there is a fine selection of bronze statuettes of all the gods. These figures have been found in large numbers near temples in the soil, which was thus consecrated by the profuse scattering in it of these divine emblems.

The theology of the Egyptians "recognizes that the universe is God, formed of several gods who compose its parts."—(Eusebius quoted by Mariette Bey). It is a species of Pantheism. One god adored throughout Egypt was Osiris. The other gods did not receive equal veneration in all parts of the country. The esoteric or hidden doctrine of the priests was that there was no plurality of gods, but, for the use of the people, the conceptions of the learned were clothed with allegorical forms. The exoteric, or external popular, doctrine taught the origin or descent of the deities who represented the forces and phenomena of nature.

The principle of light and of the creative power of nature was *kepher* or the Scarabæus, with the sun's disc, whose emblem was the sacred beetle. This sacred symbol, of which we have many examples, represents the transformation from one form to another which the good attain after the judgment of Osiris (Nos. 10465 to 10514, fifty specimens).

No. 10515. Scarab of Amenophis III. (Memnon), 18th Dynasty, 1703 to 1462 B.C.

Nos. 10516 to 10519. Four modern imitation scarabs. There is a great trade in these.

No. 10521. Scarab of Thotmes III, perhaps the most glorious of the Pharoahs or kings of Egypt.

The following are the principal gods. Where not otherwise stated, the specimen in the collection is in bronze:—

Ptah, chief of the gods (No. 10432); stone.

Ptah embryo. Represented as a dwarf (Nos. 10436 and 10434); blue porcelain.

Ra, the great god of Heliopolis or On, the Sun.

Harmachis (No. 10430), and Tum, forms of Ra (No. 10440).

Khumu, a form of Ammon, the great Trinity of Osiris, Horus and Ibis.

Osiris (Nos. 10420 and 10421), also a very fine bronze figure, No. 10423. Horus, Nos. 10403, 10407 and 10442, grey porcelain; and No. 10423, hard stone: and as a child (*Harpa-khrat*), No. 10541.

Goddess Isis, Nos. 10375, 10377 and 10404 (lapis lazuli).

Isis and Horus (No. 10408), blue porcelain; Nos. 10428 and 10442, the enemies of the above Trinity—Seth, a god, the goddess Nephthys, No. 10414, blue porcelain; Anubis, Guide of the Dead, Nos. 10433 and 10443, blue porcelain; Thoth, god of the Moon and of Learning (Nos. 10444 and 10449), green and blue porcelain.

Saket or Bast: the goddess of Passion, with the head of a cat (Nos. 10546 and 10370), blue porcelain.

Sebek (Nos. 10425 and 10427), with the head of a crocodile.

Ammon Ra—the great god of Thebes (No. 10398), green porcelain.

No. 10422, Ammon Ra—Silver; a fine specimen.

Thoueris, a goddess who appears to have presided over nursing (No. 10393), grey porcelain; Nos. 10441 and 10445, porcelain; Noum or Chnouphis, form of Ammon (No. 10440); Nofre Atmou (No. 10552), lead, very rare; son of Ptah and Seket (No. 10439), porcelain.

On the second shelf are a number of glass bottles which have become iridescent from long burial in the earth. Such bottles were used in Roman times to contain the tears of mourning friends of the dead, No. 10339 (16 in number).

There are numerous terra-cotta figures, and other objects which date from the Ptolemaic Greek period, B.C. 305—B.C. 30.

Examples of Funeral Lamps with figures in relief (Nos. 10559 to 10564).

No. 10722. Incense burner.

No. 10726. The bull Apis.

No. 10728. Horus statue.

No. 10736. Bust of a woman.

No. 10749. A camel.

No. 10738. Woman holding a tambourine.

Amongst miscellaneous objects are:—

No. 10347. The Cynocephalus monkey (baboon); sacred to Thoth.

No. 10362. A cat's head in bronze; very well modelled.

No. 10369. Sistrum, a musical instrument; a sign of mourning, broken and placed in the tombs.

No. 10525. Ring of blue porcelain of King Seti I, 19th Dynasty, 1462 to 1288 B.C.

No. 10533. Stone tablet used for casting jewellery.

No. 10537. Urœus: serpent or asp.

No. 10548. Apis or Hapi: the bull in which Osiris was supposed to be incarnate, bronze. The Greeks called him Serapis and worshipped him as a man. No. 10646 is a fine bronze bust of Serapis. No. 10647, one in terra-cotta.

No. 10575. Gnostic stone. The Gnostics were a sect who attempted to combine Greek philosophy with Christianity.

No. 10576. Bronze mirror.

No. 10577. Necklace of carnelian with amulets as pendants.

No. 10578. Gold earring.

No. 10569. Venus in gold. Greek god of Love (305 to 30 B.C.)

No. 10582. Bronze spatula.

No. 10580. Bronze spoon. A small dish of burnt clay of the 6th Dynasty from Sakarah, 5500 years old.

Nos. 10644, 10645 and 10648. Alabaster pots for ointment.

No. 10678. Male figure engraved on ivory. Greek time.

Nos. 10681 to 10691. Imitations of precious stones.

Nos. 10695 and 10696. Sacred bird: the Ibis, much revered in Egypt.

No. 10697. An intaglio model of a bird from a school for sculptors.

Nos. 10698 to 10701. Bronze bracelets and (No. 10702) scales.

Nos. 10704 to 10709. Necklaces of blue enamelled porcelain beads taken from the mummy now in the Museum.

No. 10711. A pair of sandals of the Ptolemaic time; 2000 years old.

No. 10718. Osiris; figure in wood, painted.

No. 10719. Wooden box (very rare), B.C. 1288 or 1100. Dates from 12th Dynasty.

Nos. 10542 and 10543. Two Ptolemaic bronze medals.

No. 10331. A mason's wooden mallet of the 6th Dynasty. B.C. 3703 to 3500, or about 5000 years old.

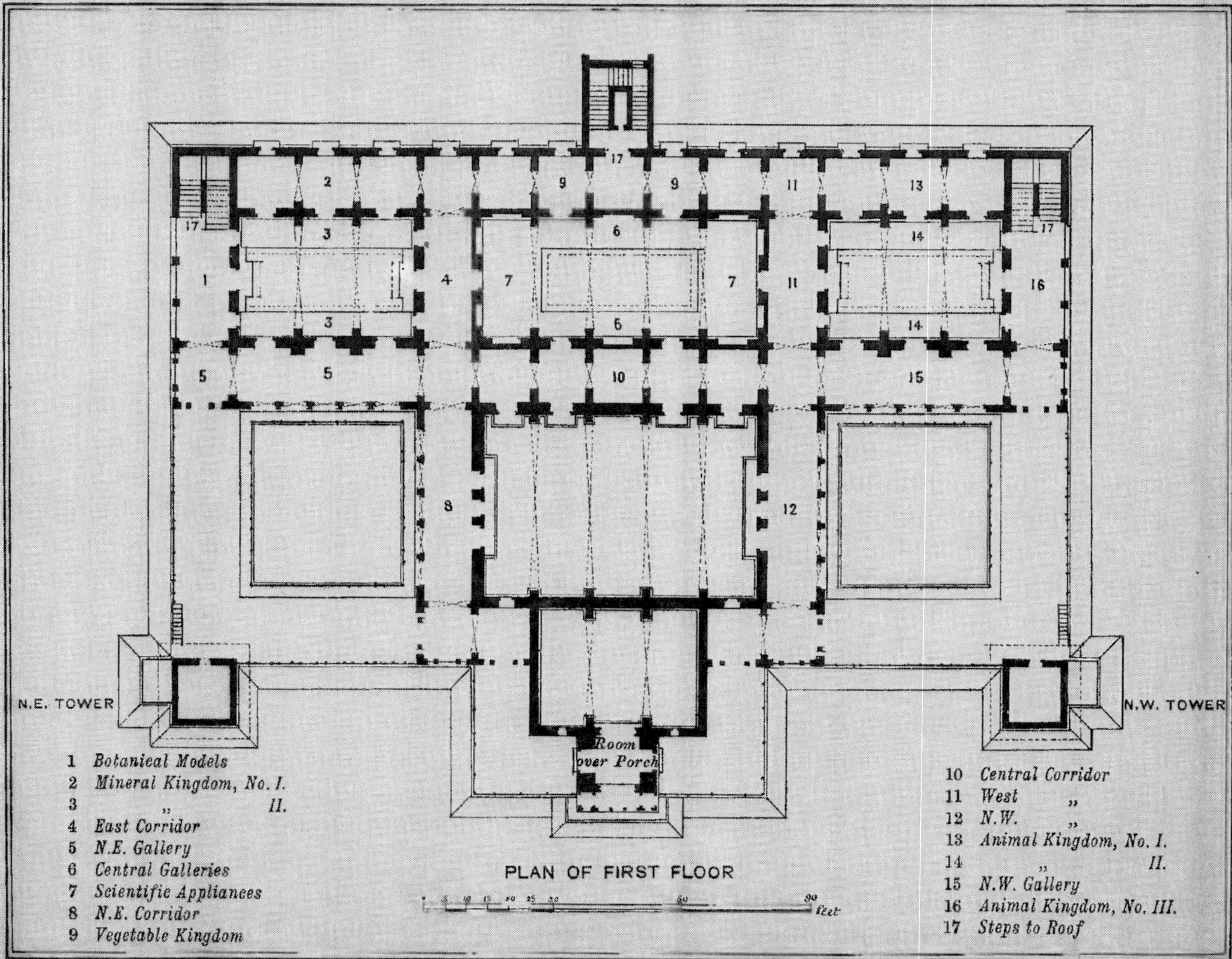

IV. JEYPORE MUSEUM, PLAN OF FIRST FLOOR.

CHAPTER XI.

PART II.—THE UPPER FLOOR OF THE MUSEUM.

The upper floor of the Museum building is devoted to the educational exhibits, and, as at present, no other accommodation is available ; it has also become necessary to add collections of commercial products, wherever room could be found for them.

Four main divisions have been formed, *viz.* :—

1. The Animal Kingdom.
2. The Vegetable Kingdom.
3. The Mineral Kingdom.
4. History, Geography, Science, &c.

No one can be more deeply sensible of the imperfection of this arrangement than I am, but, as no other building exists for the carrying out of a more perfect plan, it is necessary to make the best of the present accommodation. My own idea is that at some future time it may be possible to adopt some such scheme as the following :—

The lower floor of the present Museum may be set apart, as it mainly is at present, for the examples of industrial art and of antiquities or models which may serve to illustrate and explain them. The upper floor may contain Natural History specimens arranged as types on a pure educational basis on the lines now attempted.

In another building, perhaps connected with the present one, on the ground floor, commercial and economic products could be shown, and, in connection with them, there might be several class rooms for use in technical education. Upstairs a long gallery might be divided into separate compartments, each of which would be devoted to the display of drawings, models, casts of statues and original specimens, which should serve to illustrate the art and economic history of the world from the very earliest times. Thus, for example, the first section would contain everything which would serve to teach and illustrate the history of the Stone Age, and the next that of the Bronze Age. After these one or more sections might be reserved for Egypt, Assyria, Parthia and Persia, Ancient India, China, Japan, Arabia, Greece, the Byzantine, Roman, and Turkish Empires, Mediæval Europe, France, England, Germany, &c.

In every division the influence of the different countries and civilizations, or the growth and origin of Indian art and life, would be borne in mind, and made prominent. In this way an immense deal of knowledge would be gained, and all the collections would serve a definite purpose in educating the youth of the country, and in expanding their minds—in short, in teaching them to think instead of merely assisting in cramming them with more undigested knowledge. Much material is already available in the shape of casts from the British Museum, and of coloured drawings, photographs, models, etc., which are scattered about the rooms, but, for want of space, and consequently of systematic arrangement, much of the value of it is lost. For example, when giving a demonstration a few days ago to a party of teachers, I was compelled to wander backwards and forwards from one room to another, in order to preserve proper historical order, when I was endeavouring to illustrate the ancient histories of Egypt and Assyria by means of the numerous casts, photographs, and original examples, which are in the Museum.

With these preliminary remarks I will now proceed to a description of the collections as at present arranged, and, as it is most convenient for the visitor to begin at the west end, will commence with the Animal Kingdom, which occupies the first rooms.

At the foot of the stairs the visitor will glance at two frescoes on the walls, one representing the Emperor Justinian presenting gifts from the interior of the Church of St. Vitale at Ravenna, which dates from the sixth century; the other St. Francis, the founder of the Capuchin order of friars, preaching before Pope Honorius III, after an original in the upper church at Assisi by Giotto, the famous artist of the 13th century, with whom the modern school of art began. In this picture we see the dawnings of modern art with some imperfection of perspective still discernible. In the former we have the conventional rigidity of the Byzantine School, which so long fossilized art, which indeed was characterized by much beauty and richness of materials and delicacy of execution, but which nevertheless could never raise the thoughts of men or develop the minds of the artists. From the latter school the Indian artist has learned much, but, instead of going on to perfection, has stood still, or has even lost ground, because he has been held fast in the same swathing bands which did so much injury to the arts as practised in Byzantium and Eastern Europe. Ascending the stairs one can see a specimen of Etruscan art, which was allied to the Greek, and in a moment understand how true the above remarks are, and contrast, much in the favour of the Etruscan, his work with the stiff and formal picture from Ravenna.

In going through the educational section it will be seen that the great object has been to teach every branch of knowledge by type collections. There was no room for large accumulations of stuffed birds, beasts, and reptiles, nor would such collections have long been of any value without carefully trained naturalists to look after them; nor would a fifth-rate museum of natural history, such as alone we could have hoped to establish, have served any really useful purpose; but, when it had been once decided as to what limits should be fixed, and to have a definite scheme, the work became easy enough.

Let me take one illustration, for example—the science of Geology. We begin with three type collections—(1) Minerals, (2) Rocks, (3) Objects such as fossils, shells, etc., to illustrate a recent text-book on Geology.

The student, who takes his text book to the Museum, will find there all the principal objects, which are mentioned in those works, and of which illustrations are given. He will thus be able fairly to understand all that he reads, even unaided, and, of course with very few suggestions from a teacher, with still greater perfection. He will find close by the implements which are necessary to enable him to study his subject thoroughly; for example, in the present case (1) a box containing the specimens which form the scale of hardness of minerals, (2) the same for the scale of fusibility, (3) models of crystals,

(4) specific gravity bottles, etc. When he has mastered the elements of this particular science, he will be in a position to appreciate a more extended set of specimens from the whole Indian Empire, and, in every case, where space permits, it will be sought to complete his local education by providing for him, as far as possible, a perfect collection of objects of geological interest from the State of Jeypore or from the province of Rajputana. Beyond this it is not necessary to go in a provincial museum. With such collections, and by the aid of instruction from professors, any intelligent man could obtain a degree in the subject thus illustrated. If a man desires to become an expert, he should go to the national museum (in India to Calcutta), where nothing should be wanting, in the way of examples or professional assistance, to enable him to attain the end he has in view, though, even here, unless he has opportunities of travel, and of seeing foreign museums and countries, he can hardly expect to become an authority or teacher of the highest rank.

Throughout the rooms will be found diagrams, printed charts, or object-lessons, by which every subject is still further illustrated. For example :—

1. The Scotch series of object-lesson cards of Messrs. Oliver & Boyd of Edinburgh.

2. Similar cards, with less descriptive matter and more objects, a change for the better, of Mons. E. Deyrolle of Paris, a series which is in use in the State schools of France.

3. Cards, with excellent coloured illustrations, from Messrs. Bouasse, Lebel et Cie, of Paris ; a more advanced series than the former.

4. Miscellaneous diagrams, charts, etc., from the Agricultural College at Cirencester in England, from the Revenue and Agricultural Department in India, from reports, books, etc. ; in short, anything that would serve a useful purpose or explain a difficult point.

Lastly, special collections of local or peculiar interest are also shown ; as for example :—

1. A set of models of Bengal fishes.
2. Specimens and clay models of poisonous snakes.
3. Specimens to illustrate the silk industry.

In this way the gifts of Governments or of individuals naturally fall into their proper places in the system.

The visitor can now proceed to examine the contents of the galleries, and, in the first place, on the wall at the right hand at the top of the stairs, he will find a synoptic series of plates showing the classification of the Animal Kingdom of the Natural History Division, proceeding from the lowest forms of life to the highest. Having studied this, he enters the first door on the right and looks at the contents of the small glass cases which are attached to the gallery rails. In small gun-metal frames, which are attached to pedestals on the rail cases, will be found numerous diagrams by which the models close by are fully described and illustrated.

Herr Blaschka of Dresden has prepared a series of glass and enamelled models of specimens of animals of that great division of the Animal Kingdom which is known as the Invertebrata. They are careful studies from life, and, for general purposes, are far better than spirit preparations, which lack colour, or wax models, which, of course, are very unsuitable for exhibition in the tropics. Here will be found a number of the most useful examples, beginning with magnified specimens of the Amœba, and of the sun animalcules. The following are the principal objects, in order :—

SUB-KINGDOM I.

The Protozoa. The simplest animals, which have neither body cavity, nor nervous system, and thereby differ from the other sub-kingdoms, which possess, at some time or the other in their life history, a body cavity, and which are collectively termed Metazoa.

No. 10. Actinophrys Sol. The sun animalcule; magnified 1,000 diameters.

No. 11. Actinophrys Sol. A specimen in the state of dividing itself to form two beings instead of one.

No. 13. Amœba proteus. Two forms.

SUB-KINGDOM II.

Polystomata. Sponges which have an internal cavity with one outlet and many inlets, bounded by a bi-laminar wall.

No. 16. Corallium Rubrum. The common red coral; one portion much magnified, another the natural size.

No. 18. Alcyonium digitatum, dead man's fingers.

No. 21. Pennatula phosphorea, or the sea pen.

Sea anemones, such as—

No. 28. Anthea Cereus.

No. 30. Actinia.

Nos. 32 to 34. Sagartia. They are called animal flowers and sea anemones, and were long thought to belong to the Vegetable Kingdom. Group No. 41 shows a struggle of two Actiniœ. In an aquarium, for example, a Mesembryanthemum and Sagartia, if kept together, may fight with each other. The former will attack the latter with its nettling batteries, and the latter retorts with its acontia or missile cords, which are filled with nettling capsules charged with nettling threads. The group is well worth patient study.

No. 48. The Girdle of Venus, or Cœstum Veneris, which appears like a waving flame in the sea at night.

A number of models of Jelly fishes and a fine group of Sea Anemones will be found in Case No. 110 in the outermost gallery. They belong to Sub-kingdom III, Cœlenterata.

The Echinodermata, Sub-kingdom IV, Star fishes, follow. They are radiated, and have a body-cavity, separate from the stomach, a nervous system, and a system of water tubes, which are agents in locomotion.

Amongst these are :—

Nos. 50 to 52. Asteracanthion Palidus.

No. 53. Comatula Hamata. Rosy feather star.

No. 55. Ophiomastix.

No. 56. Ophiothrix Fragilis, Annulosa.

No 59. Holothuria Edulis. The edible trepang, a luxury of diet in China.

SUB-KINGDOM V.—VERMES: WORMS,

Which are bilaterally symmetrical, and composed of successive similar segments, with no jointed limbs, and with a water vascular system, which has no locomotary function.

No. 85. Arenicola Marnia. The lob-worm used as bait.

No. 86. Hirudo Medicinalis. The leech, natural size, and enlarged, to show the anatomy.

Nos. 87 to 89. Autolytus Cornutus. Showing five stages of development.

SUB-KINGDOM VI.—MOLLUSCA.

Oysters, snails, etc., possessing soft bodies enveloped in a leathery mantle, unjointed limbs, a circulating system, often an external shell, and an unsymmetrical nervous system.

No. 97. Lima Squamosa.

No. 98. Cardium Edule. The cockle.

No. 99. Mytilus Edulis. The mussel in the living state (cut out from the shell), and opened to show its anatomy.

No. 100. Pecten Opercularis. Razor shell, Scallop-shells. (1) Living state, (2) dissected.

No. 102. Solen Vagina.

No. 104. Venus Gallina. Natural state.

No. 105. Venus Gallina. Dissected.

No. 107. Vola Jacobœa. (1) Living state, (2) dissected.

No. 135. Melibe Fimbriata.

No. 142. Doris Arbutus.

No. 143. Doris Fragilis.

No. 149. Aplysia Inca. The sea-hare.

No. 156. Turbo Rugosus.

No. 160. Clausilia Bidens. (1) Living state, (2) dissected.

No. 161. Murex Brandaris : (1) Natural size, living state, (2) dissected.

No. 162. Cerithium Vulgatum (Spirula). (1) Living state, (2) dissected.

No. 168. Arion Empiricorum. (1) Living state, (2) anatomy.

No. 169. Helix Pomatia. Dissected.

No. 170. Limax Agrestis. The slug.

No. 171. Helix Pomatia.

No. 172. Helix Hortensis. The garden snail.

No. 177. Succinea Amphibia. (1) Living state, (2) dissected.

No. 178. Argonauta Argo.

No. 181. Ditto.

No. 184. Loligo Vulgaris. The squid.

No. 186. Loligopsis Vermicularis.

No. 187. Octopus Macropus.

No. 188. Octopus Vulgaris. The devil fish.

No. 193. Sepia Officinalis. The Sepia or cuttle fish.

No. 194. The Sepia. Dissected.
No. 202. Ciona Fascicularis.
No. 208. Bolteria Burkhardii.
No. 209. Pyrosoma Atlanticum.
No. 211. Sulpa Africana Maxima.
No. 213. Salpa Ferruginea.

The Mollusca having been illustrated, it is natural to proceed to the houses in which most of them live, and so to the science of shells or Conchology.

Nos. 214 to 313 form a collection for teaching the nomenclature of the shells and are followed by a selection of Indian shells generally (Nos. 314 to 493). For further study a larger collection has been placed in drawers in the West Gallery.

The next case contains (for convenience of position only) a fairly complete collection of the eggs of birds which live in Rajputana (Nos. 494 to 567). On the wall are two plates (No. 569): (1) of eggs of domestic fowls, (No. 568) (2) of nests of birds from all parts of the world.

Plates Nos. 570, 572 and 573. Classification of birds, articulated animals and zoophytes, explained by means of coloured drawings of their heads and claws. Beyond this are plates showing the anatomy and classification of insects, and, on the walls of the adjacent galleries, are many more drawings of the same kind, with a large illustrative collection, in wall frames, of insects from the Eastern Hemisphere.

We now proceed to Case No. 110 in the West gallery, which contains, first, a series of glass models of jelly fish (Nos. 1116 to 1138), a group of sea anemones in the same material, and specimens to illustrate the study of the Vertebrata, or the highest division of the animal kingdom. Each of the classes of fish, reptiles, and birds is represented (in most cases in their natural surroundings) by a well-known specimen, and in some cases by skeletons. Dissected examples and models are also exhibited to show the anatomy of the different divisions. For example, in the case of the birds, a common turkey (No. 1184) is shown, and close beside a skeleton of it (No. 1185), and then a model (No. 1186), which was made in Paris of *papier mache*, and which displays all the internal organs, the muscles, arteries, veins, nerves, and other structures in such a way that the student can compare them with similar parts in fishes, reptiles, or in animals, and thus see what modifications have been made to adapt the bird to the special condition of its life in the air.

A collection of this kind is far more valuable than a miscellaneous assortment of fishes, reptiles, birds, or beasts, such as is generally found in small Natural History museums. The following is a complete list of the contents of the case :—

SPECIMENS OF JELLY FISH AND SEA ANEMONES.—NOS. 1116 TO 1138.

(INVERTEBRATA: SUB-KINGDOM VII.)

Arthropoda.—Crabs, lobsters, spiders and insects, which have bodies made up of successive segments, with a symmetrical nervous system or external skeleton (chitinous or like horn) or calcified (like chalk), and jointed limbs.

The insects are arranged on the walls in frames.

No. 1139 is a large crab or lobster.

VERTEBRATA.

The vertebrata include fishes, reptiles, birds, and quadrupeds, which have an internal skeleton, a brain, and a vertebral column or back-bone. They are divided into classes.

CLASS I.—FISHES.

The first and simplest of head-bearing vertebrates.

Order I.—Marsipobranchii (Lampreys)—Fish with pouch-like gills.

No. 1141. The Lamprey.

Order II.—Elasmobranchii (Sharks)—Fishes with symmetrical lateral pouches for gills.

No. 1142. The dog fish.

Order III.—Ganoidei (Ganoid fishes)—Fishes with polished scales covered with enamel.

No. 1443. The Sturgeon.

Order IV.—Teleostei (Bony Fishes).

Sub-order I.—Physostomi—Fishes in which the swimming bladder, in the adult, opens into the digestive canal by a duct.

No. 1444. The Herring.

Sub-order II.—Anacanthini—The soft-finned fishes, either with no swimming bladder, or with one without a duct.

No. 1145. The Sole.

Sub-order III.—Acanthopteri—Spiny-finned fishes: The Mackerel, Perch, etc.

No. 1145. The Perch. Stuffed specimen.
No. 1147. The Perch. Skeleton.
No. 1148. Dissected specimen of a fresh fish.
No. 1149. The Carp: clay model.
No. 1150. The Mackerel. Skeleton.
No. 1151. The Mackerel. Stuffed.

Sub-order IV.—Pharyngognathi—Pharynx-jaw-bearing fishes.

No. 1152. The Belone.

Sub-order V.—Laphobranchii, or tufted-gilled fishes.

No. 1153. The Syngnathus.

Sub-order VI.—Plectognathi or soldered jaws.

No. 1154. The Balister.

Order V.—Dipnoi—The swimming bladder becomes an accessory respiratory organ.

No. 1155. The Protopterus, or African mud fish.

No. 1140. A disarticulated, and beautifully mounted, skull of the codfish showing all the bones, which are capable of being removed in groups.

Class II.—Vertebrata—Amphibia.

Cold-blooded animals.

Order I.—Gymnophiona—Worm-like forms without limbs.

No. 1156. The Anguis.

Order II.—Urodela—Limb-bearing. Amphibious: living in water and on the land.

No. 1157. The Axolotl of Mexico.

Order III.—Anura—The tail-less form. Frogs, etc.

No. 1158. The frog, stuffed specimen.

No. 1159. Skeleton of a frog.

Class III.

Reptilia (Reptiles): Cold-blooded Animals.

Order I.—Lacertilia—Lizards.

No. 1161. The lizard, stuffed.

No. 1160. Fresh lizard in spirit.

Order II.—Ophidia—Snakes.

No. 1162. Vipera Aspis.

No. 1163. A common snake preserved in spirit.

No. 1164. The skeleton of a snake to illustrate the osteology of the Reptilia.

Order III.—Chelonia—Tortoises.

No. 1165. Turtle, clay model.

No. 1166. Dissected tortoise in spirit.

Order IV.—Crocodilia—Crocodiles.

No. 1167. Crocodile, clay model.

Class IV.

Aves (Birds): Warm-blooded animals without teeth, adapted for aërial locomotion.

Sub-class I.—Ratitœ, or without a keel on the breast-bone.

Order I.—The cassowary—The ostrich—The emu.

No. 1168. Ostrich. Model in clay.

Sub-class II.—Carinatœ (with a keel on the breast-bone).

Order I.—Psittaci—Parrots. The most intelligent birds.

No. 1172. The parrot.

No. 1170. Skeleton of a parrot.

No. 1171. Dissected specimen of a bird in spirit.

No. 1169. Disarticulated skull of a fowl. (*Gallus domesticus:* the common cock.)

Order II.—Coccygomorphœ (Cuckoos), the Cuckoo—The Hoopoe.

No. 1173. The Kingfisher.

Order III.—Pici : Woodpeckers.

No. 1174. The Woodpecker.

Order IV.—Macrochires—Swifts and Humming Birds.

No. 1175. The goat-sucker.

No. 1176. The Swift.

Order V.—Paseres—Perching Birds.

No. 1177. The nightingale.

No. 1178. The crow.

No. 1179. Pica Caudata.

No. 1180. The crow; clay model

No. 1181. The cock ; clay model.

Order VI.—Raptores—Birds of Prey : The owl ; the hawk ; the eagle ; the vulture.

No. 1182. The Condor, clay model.

Order VII.—Gyrantes—Pigeons.

No. 1183. The pigeon.

Order VIII.—Rasores—Scraping birds.

No. 1184. The common turkey, stuffed.

No. 1185. The skeleton of a turkey.

No. 1186. Model of a turkey showing the internal organs and anatomy. The hollow bones and cells, which are filled with air, can be well seen.

Order IX.—Gralloe—The waders. The heron.

Order X.—Cicoinoe—The stork.

No. 1187. The Ibis.

Order XI.—Lamellirostres—Ducks and geese.

No. 1188. The Teal.

Order XII.—Longipennes—Long-winged birds.

No. 1189. The common gull.

Order XIII.—Steganopodes—Pelicans.

No. 1191. The pelican. In Case No. 151.

Order XIV.—Pygopodes—The Penguins.

No. 1190. The penguin.

N.B.—The orders will be also illustrated by Indian birds, if possible.

One small case, No. 113, is filled with a representative collection of stuffed and varnished fresh-water fish of (Nos. 1193 to 1222) Rajputana, and on the wall near it is a frame No. 112 showing the development of the trout fish from the ovum up to the complete animal.

No. 1192. This is one of the excellent specimens prepared by Mons. Deyrolle of Paris.

CASE NO. 114.

The long case in the centre of the gallery contains models to show how the processes of life are carried on in all branches of the animal kingdom. In short, the science of comparative anatomy is here taught in the most graphic manner. As the lowest animals are simply stomachs, it is natural to begin with that organ, hence we have the following examples :—

Stomachs of a bee; of a locust; of an octopus; of a cray fish; of a dog fish (with intestine); of an owl, a bird of prey; of a rodent or gnawing animal, such as the rat; of a horse of the class solidungula, that is of animals having solid hoofs; of a lion—or carnivorous, that is a flesh-eating, animal; of a gramnivorous or gram-feeding bird (the common fowl); of a ruminant, which chews its food twice over, as a sheep; of the human being, an omnivorous animal, or one who eats every kind of food.

Nos. 1223 to 1234. In another model a front view of the human stomach is shown, and beside it a back view of the same (No. 1235).

No. 1236 is a model of a digestive system of a cockroach.

No. 1237 is a section of a portion of the human body showing the whole of the digestive system. The function of the digestive organs is to elaborate the blood, hence we naturally come to the organs of circulation, of which the following specimens are shown.

The heart and blood vessels of the Doris (a Cephalopodous mollusk); of a mussel; of a cuttle fish; of a carp; of an oyster; of a dugong (a swimming mammal of the Indian Ocean); of a turtle; of a serpent; of a crocodile; of a human infant just before birth (enlarged); and of a man (Nos. 1238 to 1248).

The controlling or nervous system comes next, with the models noted below :—

The nervous system of an articulated animal in three stages, *viz.* (1) the larva, (2) the pupa or chrysalis, and (3) the perfect insect; of a cray fish; of a spider; of a starfish (a radiated animal); and of a mollusc (Nos. 1250 to 1254); the brains of a skate fish; of a carp; of a viper; of a turtle; of a goose; of a cat (carnivorous animal); and of a rat or rodent animal (Nos. 1263 to 1269).

The cerebellum, or lesser brain of man, with the medulla oblongata and the spinal cord with the origins of the spinal nerves (No. 1270).

The brain of man divided so as to show its different parts and the origin of the cranial nerves (No. 1271). The brain of man, natural size, undivided (No. 1272).

Then comes the respiratory system, illustrated by the lungs and vocal cords of a frog (No. 1256); the wind-pipe (trachea), air sacs, and heart of an insect, a bug (both magnified), No. 1255; the larynx (voice box), lungs, and air sacs of a bird (No. 1257).

The muscular and osseous systems are illustrated by a model of the flayed arm of a man showing the superficial muscles (No. 1259), and by the dissected specimen of a small mammal, *viz.*, the rabbit (No. 1249) with its skeleton (No. 1261), and the excretory organs by models of (No. 1258) the human kidneys, the left divided to show the construction (No. 1277), and a magnified section of the human skin, showing the hair bulbs, sweat, and sebaceous glands and ducts.

The organs of special sense, which follow, are illustrated by beautiful models on a very large scale.

V. A SHOW CASE.

No. 1276. Of the throat or organ of voice.

No. 1275. Half the human head, showing the parts at the base of the skull, the eye, the ear, the nasal cavities, the mouth, the tongue, the gullet and the organ of voice;—or the organs of sight, hearing, smell, taste, and voice.

No. 1273. The human ear, showing its minute construction.

No. 1274. The eye, showing the muscles, vessels, nerves, membranes, and humours.

Most of the above models can be separated into numerous parts to display the minute anatomy.

No. 1260. Model of the human hand.

No. 1262 is an enlarged model of a scorpion after Huxley.

Lastly, when the individual is complete, the next act in life is the reproduction of another individual, which is here shewn by—

1. A frame containing small wax models which show the growth of the bird from the first stage in the egg to the last, and then the complete chicken (No. 1279).

2. An enormously enlarged egg, the size of that of the extinct epyornis, which, in four sections, displays the development of the chick, in different stages, *viz.*, at the 1st, 5th, 12th, and 18th days of incubation (No. 1278). On the adjacent wall is a diagram of the same giving further details, and near to it are many other drawings, which serve to still further explain and amplify the instruction conveyed in the beautiful models in the case, most of which were made by Mons. Auzoux, of Paris, though there are others, less artistic but otherwise equally valuable, which come from Berlin. The Paris models can be taken to pieces, and are really almost as valuable to students of anatomy, as if they made fresh dissections for themselves. In the adjacent small case are the following objects:—

First, sets of the bones of a mammal (a cat : No. 1280), a bird (a duck: No. 1281); and a fish (a cod : No. 1282), which are arranged on a board, in corresponding positions, so as to show the modifications of the different bones in the different animals to suit them, respectively, for progression on the earth, in the air, and in the water. There are two very much magnified models of a silkworm (No. 1283), and a snail (No. 1284), which are intended to show the wonderful elaboration of parts to the end in view, even in some of the smallest members of the animal world. In short, we are here taught the element of design in creation; an element which, according to the address of the Marquis of Salisbury, as President of the British Association at Oxford in 1894, seems to be coming once more prominently to the front even amongst scientists. This may be further studied in the specimens preserved in spirit, which illustrate the metamorphoses of the frog (No. 1285), of the newt (No. 1286), of the beetle (No. 1287), of the wasp (No. 1288), and of the bee (No. 1289); and again, on the north wall close by, in the set of well-executed models of the different stages in the growth of the tadpole and frog (No. 1290). On the opposite wall, amongst the drawings, the most interesting are :—

A magnified drop of water (No. 1293), and a synoptic table illustrative of sericulture.

The adjacent frames contain a complete collection to illustrate sericulture in India (silkworms, cocoons, etc.—Nos. 1296 to 1310).

The drawings on the adjacent wall form portions of a set of object lessons for elementary schools. They are in use throughout France, and have been published by Messieurs Deyrole et Cie in English, in the hope that they will be equally useful in Great Britain.

Sufficient space is not available to represent the mammalia, or the highest class of warm-blooded animals, by means of large stuffed specimens; nor is it necessary, because the adjacent Gardens contain a large zoological collection which amply illustrates the subject; but, in a small Case No. 141, a number of felt models of animals, in proper proportion as regards size, is placed so that there may not appear to be a gap in the Museum exhibits (Nos. 1323 to 1362). Close by are maps of the distribution of the Animal Kingdom (Nos. 1363 to 1368), drawings of the horns and teeth of animals (Nos. 1369 to 1371), and a few Indian horns, which afford further subjects of study.

In a large Case No. 151, which fills up the centre of the gallery, are the following important objects:—Dissected model of a cow's foot (No. 1384); model of the sound leg of a horse (No. 1385); the same with the skin removed, to show the anatomy (No. 1386); a leg showing the bony tumours (No. 1387); a leg, with separate removable parts, to show the different bony tumours, which are known as spavins, jardes, curbs, splints, and ringbones (No. 1388); a leg with the skin removed, showing the soft tumours (No. 1389); the bones of the leg (No. 1390); the foot of the horse, showing the minute anatomy (No. 1391); and, lastly, a large model of a horse (Arab type), showing the anatomy, which can be separated into 97 pieces for teaching purposes (No. 1392). This specimen cost £48. These models are of great value for teaching a veterinary class. Model of a man (about the height of a boy of 14 years of age) of a similar character to that of the horse (No. 1393).

The following stuffed birds, &c., which were too large for Case No. 110:—

Perca fluviatilis (No. 1394).

Vespertilis murinus (No. 1395).

Singnathus, a stuffed fish (No. 1396).

A heron (No. 1397).

A kite (No. 1398).

A manikin of cardboard with folding parts, to shew the construction of the human body (No. 1400). In the extreme right-hand corner of the gallery on the wall are:—

(1) Models showing the dentition of the horse at different ages (No. 1433); (2) diagrams of (*a*) the anatomy of the ox (No. 1432), (*b*) of the horse (No. 1428), and (*c*) of his defects (No. 1430), and (*d*) of the age of the horse, ox, sheep, and dog (No. 1429). Object lessons from the mammalia.

Case No. 152.

In the last case in the room are some excellent models of animals which existed before man appeared on the earth. These help to illustrate the science of palæontology, or the science of the ancient life of the earth. These animals are known from their fossil remains, and their forms are conjectural. The following is a complete list of them:—

Ramphorhynchus—a flying lizard with hollow bones and a long tail (No. 1402).

Sivatherium giganteum—a huge giraffe-like beast, of which the remains were found in the Siwalik Hills in India in the older pliocene formation. It was a ruminant (No. 1403).

Rhinoceros Trichorhynus—the woolly rhinoceros. Its body has been found frozen in Siberia (No. 1404).

Mastodon Longirostris (found in India)—eleven feet high in some cases. Remains obtained from the miocene tertiary formation (No. 1045).

Iguanodon—a great extinct land reptile about 30 feet long; a vegetarian. From the wealden formation (No. 1406).

Pterodactylus—a flying lizard from the Solenhofen limestone, the great oolite beds, and the lias. Lived in the jurassic age (No. 1407).

Megalosaurus—a carnivorous animal, from the oolite beds (No. 1408).

Anoplotherium—a ruminant, from the lower miocene formation (No. 1409).

Ichthyosaurus—a short-necked marine fish lizard 22 feet long; the shark of the old classic seas (No. 1410).

Archœopterix lithographica—the long-tailed fossil bird; from the lithographic stone in Bavaria, the oldest fossil bird known (No. 1411).

Hylœosaurus—a huge plated lizard; an armed land reptile with formidable spines on its back; from the wealden formation; perhaps amphibious (No. 1412).

Dinotherium giganteum—an animal like an elephant, with tusk-like teeth in the lower jaw; from the upper miocene formation (No. 1414).

Mastodonsaurus robustus (No. 1415).

Plesiosaurus dolichodeirus—a long-necked sea lizard; from the lias; its jaw was six feet long and paddle seven feet in length (No. 1416).

Nicrosaurus (No. 1417).

Anchitherium—an early ancestor of the horse; from the miocene formation (No. 1418).

Dinoceros mirabile—a huge herbivorous animal; from the eocene formation (No. 1419).

Cervus megaceros—the gigantic Irish deer; found in peat bogs in Ireland; its antlers sometimes spread nine feet across (No. 1420).

Elephas primogenius—the mammoth elephant, of which specimens, even with the skin and flesh, have been found frozen in North Siberia (No. 1421).

The collection is completed by a few bones of the extinct bird the Dinornis, from New Zealand (Nos. 1422, 1423, 1424 and 1425), which were presented by Surg.-Lieut.-Colonel Johnson, I.M.D., and a coprolite, or nodule formed of phosphate of lime, which is supposed to be excrementitions and to have been formed by fish and reptiles of the geological chalk marls, green sands, &c. (No. 1426).

The south end of the same gallery contains a large carved wooden door from Bhera in the Punjab (No. 1443); a window from Shekhawati (No. 1492), four carved brackets from Shekhawati (Nos. 1483 and 1484), Kapurthala (No. 1485) and Saharanpur (Nos. 1486 to 1488); perforated wooden panels and *pinjra* work from the Punjab (Nos. 1489 to 1492 with two panels (Nos. 1494 to 1495); two Burmese candlesticks (Nos. 1496 and 1497); a set of old wooden blocks, for printing chintz patterns, from Sanganir, near Jeypore (Nos. 1498 to 1527); another set for printing floor cloths (Nos. 1444 to 1482); a carved wood panel copied from the original, which was made at Lahore for H.R.H. the Duke of Connaught (No. 1442); and a case of dried South Indian fishes.

On the walls are Japanese paintings. Wall Frames Nos. 176, 179, 191, 192, 197, 198, 203 and 206.

Coloured plates of the Bouasse Lebel Series of:—

1. Ornamental foliage in Wall Frames Nos. 199, 200 and 201.

2. Useful plants in Wall Frames Nos. 202 and 204, fruit, &c., and also Nos. 193, 194, 195 and 196.

3. Of systematic botany, in Wall Frames Nos. 205, 207 and 208, shewing the morphology, nomenclature, and classification of plants.

The frames in a revolving pillar frame (No. 175) at the south end of this gallery are filled with copies by the Arundel Society of works of the best of the old Italian Masters, and with reproductions of drawings by them. The latter were presented by the Trustees of the British Museum. There are also *fac-simile* reproductions of the handwriting of distinguished persons.

The room on the south at the back of the gallery just described is chiefly devoted to special collections, and the shelves on its walls and those also of the main hall are filled with bottles of economic products from the animal kingdom, which are found in Rajputana. The case No. 212 contains painted clay models of Bengal fishes, another No. 232, two sets of snakes, one of well-made models of the principal poisonous snakes of India, the other of specimens in spirit. In the last Case No. 232 is an enlarged Paris model showing the poison apparatus of a venomous serpent.

In the central Case No. 245 are clay models of nearly all the different tradesmen in Jeypore who work on animal products. These models prove attractive especially to Indian visitors.

CHAPTER XII.

VEGETABLE KINGDOM.

RETURNING by the revolving frames lately described, the rooms devoted to the vegetable kingdom are entered. Rajputana vegetable products fill the bottles in the wall cases (Nos. 307, 308, 315, 316, 323 to 325, 332, 333, and 340 to 342), and a set of clay models of workers in those products will be found in the centre case (No. 261). The side cases (Nos. 258 and 259, 260 and 262), contain clay models from Poona, Krishnagar, Lucknow, and Jeypore, of boats, figures of men and women of different castes, nationalities, professions, and occupations. On the walls are diagrams, object-lesson cards, &c., connected with the subjects of botany and of the weather on which both so much depend (Nos. 263 to 301). The galleries round the main hall of the building, which are entered from the last room, have, in the rail cases, collections of clay models of fruit and vegetables which were made in Lucknow, Trichinopoly, Jeypore, &c., of fodder grasses of North India (Cases Nos. 382 to 396), of antiquities which were found near the Sambhur lake on an old Buddhist site (No. 400), with small sets of the vegetable poisons, and of the mineral elements (Case No. 399). At the ends of the galleries are two broad spaces, in which are arranged in three cases a valuable collection of scientific apparatus and models of machinery (Nos. 418, 420 and 421).*

A long corridor at the back of this room is filled with models of buildings, and with casts of many of the principal examples of the famous sculptures of the Indo-Bactrian Kingdom of the Punjab which are now in the Lahore Museum. At the south end of the east corridor is a revolving pillar with frames which contain plates to illustrate.

I. No. 426. Dr. Rudolf Menze's introduction to ancient art in the following divisions :—

Egyptian art ; Chaldean, Assyrian, Phœnician, and Cyprian art ; Persian art ; Cyprian and pre-Hellenic art ; Greek art ; art among the Romans ; lesser arts among the Greeks and Romans.

II. Plates from the Graphic arts by P. Hammerton, by which the different methods of illustrating books by engraving, pen and ink, charcoal, chalk, and pencil are shown.

III. A few specimens of the fine photographs of Braun and Cie, of Paris, selected from the great masters.

IV. A series of portraits of British worthies of the past three hundred years, including sovereigns, viceroys, statesmen, poets, philosophers, artists, clergymen, doctors, lawyers, artists, and literary men.

V. A series of coins of great sovereigns, which are exhibited as actual portraits of men who have ruled mighty empires. They begin with Alexander the Great and end with Napoleon I.

* These, and a few minerals which are kept in drawers, were all that remained of collections which belonged to the School of Art and to an old museum, which existed for a few years in the time of the late Maharajah of Jeypore, but which was closed by him in his lifetime.

CHAPTER XIII.

MINERAL KINGDOM.

WE now proceed to the collections from the mineral kingdom. Near the window is a case of specimens of salt from the Rajputana salt sources at Sambhar, Phalaudi, Didwana, and Pachbadra, and from the salt mines in the Punjab.

The next case (No. 436) contains a series of models of precious stones, and of the largest diamonds in the world, goedes, agates, enamels, and near it (in Case No. 437) are a model of the "Welcome" gold nugget and the appliances for studying mineralogy. Case No. 439 is a case of the products of Ajmere. It forms the official collection of that district, and is placed here by order of the Government of India. On the walls are, first, a chromo-lithographic *fac-simile* of the Papyrus of Ani (the Book of the Dead) which was presented by the British Museum trustees (Wall Frames Nos. 441 to 446); second, a comparative historical chronological chart of the Rajputana Princes which was compiled by Munshi Jawala Sahai of Jeypore (Wall Frames Nos. 451 and 452), and some object-lesson cards; the most instructive of these are four, which show the history of the earth from the earliest period, by means of diagrams, printed explanations, specimens of minerals, rocks, and fossils (Frames Nos. 455 to 458). Others in the same graphic way describe the manufacture of pottery and glass (Nos. 459 to 462), and, in the next or south room, are articles made of lead, zinc, copper, iron, steel, &c. High above the latter are boards, to which are fastened the tools of all kinds, which are used by blacksmiths and carpenters (Nos. 464 to 467). The first (Case No. 463) in this room contains, in a number of bottles, the constituent parts, in a pound or pint, of all the common articles of food, thus illustrating in a graphic manner, such as no tables can possibly do, the reasons why vegetarians and flesh-eaters are both able to preserve life from apparently very dissimilar, and often, as it would appear, unsuitable substances.

Here we have the water, nitrogenous matter, starch, or sugar, and mineral constituents of a pint of milk or a pound of fresh eggs, of mutton and fish, of grains, and of condiments of all kinds.

In the next case (No. 474) are clay models of workers in mineral products forming a large and most interesting collection.

In the last case (No. 481) are two sets of glass models of crystals, and bottles filled with salts, showing all the natural forms which crystals assume, thus illustrating the science of crystalography. Round the walls are bottles and tins filled with mineral products.

The adjacent galleries contain on the rail cases (Nos. 513 to 526):—

1. A type collection of British rocks.
2. A type collection of minerals.
3. A collection to illustrate recent writers on geology.
4. Special collections of emeralds in the matrix; silver ores from Australia; agates from Oberstein; building stones from Udaipur, Ulwar, Jeypore and Ajmere.

In the Wall Frames Nos. 539 to 542 are mineral products, and on the walls drawings and diagrams (Nos. 543 to 563) illustrative of the mineral kingdom, reproductions from the Ajunta cave frescoes, and some cards (presented by Mr. Lord of Birmingham), which show how a combination pocket knife, a pin, a needle, a hair-pin, and a pen are made. On leaving the room by the most westerly door on the north side we find, in a frame (No. 564), similar sets of specimens to illustrate the manufacture of a tin plate, a file, a hammer, an oil-can body, and a cash bowl. We now enter the corridor, which is devoted to science, history, and geography, and here we have, in order, diagrams of scales of colour (Nos. 565 to 610); astronomical charts; a great chronological chart of the history of the world; plates illustrating heraldry; the history of architecture; the commerce and trade of the world; a complete series of Indian maps which deal with the geography, history, languages, trade, meteorology, &c., of India, and a set of relief maps of the principal countries of the world. In the frames of a large pillar (No. 615) and in some frames in the gallery are placed a beautiful set of oleographs by Hoeltz of Vienna.

The first series illustrate the great natural phenomena of the world, as for example the cañons of North America, the pink terraces of New Zealand, a mangrove swamp of the North Cape, and the Himalaya Mountains, amongst which towers Kinchinjinga, the glaciers of the Rhine and Vesuvius. The second series represent the work of man on the globe, as shewn by his buildings, *viz.*, the pyramids and other Egyptian structures, the Assyrian remains, the magnificent relics of ancient Greece and Rome, the Churches of Saint Sophia and St. Peter's, with the town halls, palaces, and cathedrals of Europe, and the mosques of Cairo, &c. Beyond this is a large case (No. 616), in which are a complete collection of apparatus, termed "the scientific schoolmaster's set"; the model of a British India steamer, presented by the Marquis of Ailsa; a relief globe; drawing models; and a collection of metallic ores, and also the model of an unsanitary Indian house. In the next case (No. 617) are some casts of small objects from the British Museum, *e.g.*, the Portland vase, a Chaldean gate socket, the deluge tablet, a collection of seals, amongst them one of Darius the Great King, the oldest inscribed stone in the British Museum, which is supposed to be the top of the sceptre of Sargon I of Agade, who lived B.C. 3500, and portions of the bronze gates of Balawat.

There are also a new cylinder of Nebuchadnezzar, an Assyrian weight, and two pretty little casts of a tragic mask, and a Bacchante from ancient Greece.

In the last case in this gallery are all the apparatus and materials which are necessary to illustrate a lecture on Hygiene and all the objects used in the object cards of Messrs. Oliver & Boyd of Edinburgh, and on the elementary cards of Mons. Deyrolle of Paris.

Returning to the North Gallery we find the first case (No. 619), which contains clay models representing men and women indulging in Indian luxuries of different kinds, such as smoking tobacco or the poppy, drinking wine, or infusion of Indian hemp, eating opium, dancing, playing cards, &c. The great central case (No. 620) is devoted to religion. It is filled with groups of figures showing the worship, in Shivaite or Visnavi temples, or of men and women at caste feasts, separate figures of gods and men and devotees in every possible position, some lying on beds of stones or spikes, others with withered arms or iegs, and many who are seated in contemplation in the *asans* or positions described in works on philosophy, religion, and mysticism. No case attracts greater attention than this of both European and Indian visitors. In the next case (No. 621) is a group of figures of Mohamedans, who are taking out a *tazia* or model of the tomb of Hassan and Hussein at Karbela at the time of Moharrum. There are also models showing the manner in which thugs used to decoy and kill their victims.

The last great case (No. 628) in the upper story is devoted to the teaching of botany Here are dissected models of flowers, of fruits, and of the stem of a tree, of all the modes of grafting fruit trees, of ornamental gourds, and of specimens of Jeypore useful woods. On the walls are models of flowers, by Madame Jauch, of Breslau, of many of the plants, which yield drugs, that are used in medicine, and on the wall, opposite the case of Religious Models, will be found diagrams and object-lesson cards connected with the vegetable kingdom, and copies of the Magna Carta, and of Shakespeare's deeds. Throughout these upper rooms, scattered here and there, are cases of textiles from different parts of Rajputana.

On the sides of the staircase are two paintings of the great winged bull and lion of Assyria, and passing these we reach the entrance turnstile, and so complete the tour of the Museum.

FINIS.